PERMANENT LOVE:

Practical Steps
to a Lasting Relationship

by
Edward E. Ford
and
Steven Englund

[handwritten inscription and signatures, dated 7/22/81]

OTHER BOOKS BY THE AUTHORS:

by Edward E. Ford

Why Marriage?
Why Be Lonely?

by Edward E. Ford and Steven Englund

For the Love of Children

Copyright ©1979, Edward E. Ford and Steven Englund.
All rights reserved. No part of this book
may be reproduced or used in any form without
written permission from Winston Press, Inc.

Library of Congress Catalog Card Number: 78-78374

ISBN (paper): 0-03-051216-6
ISBN (cloth): 0-03-052696-5

Printed in the United States of America

5 4 3 2

Winston Press, Inc.
430 Oak Grove
Minneapolis, Minnesota 55403

For Hester
in our twenty-ninth year of marriage

For Michelle

*"In those matters seemingly
removed from love, the feeling is
secretly to be found, and man
cannot possibly live for a moment
without it."*   Pascal
Discours sur les passions de l'amour

PREFACE

In an age of gimmicks and short-cuts, much of it parading under the label of "self-help," it is a somewhat thankless task to swim against the current, and even try, upon occasion, to reverse it. Yet that is the intention of this little book on love. Where genuine loving is concerned—unlike weight loss or physical fitness—there are no tricks and abbreviations, no means provided by technological society and its psychology, to make for an easy way to success.

There is no easy path to love any more than there is an easy path through life; and indeed the comparison is apt, for loving is essentially an expression of daily living, not the dreamy-eyed creation of romance foisted off on Western society in the late eleventh century by bards and troubadours. So great are the misperceptions and distortions engendered by current notions of romantic love that, to be blunt, permanent love is increasingly beyond the attainment of many people.

The intent of this book is to offer a calm, reasonable antidote to the ravages and caricatures of loving with which romantic love has saddled our culture. We are not theorists, however. Fundamentally, from first to last, we have tried to write a practical book. The four steps which follow—tested again and again in Ed's counseling practice, and in the personal lives of both authors—are simply one means of putting people back in touch with the underlying material and psychological realities on which true romantic (or any kind of) love ultimately rests.

Finally, of course, there is no absolute insurance for anyone, authors and reader alike, that permanent love can be achieved this side of paradise. As C. S. Lewis noted in his splendid essay *The Four Loves,* * "We find thus by experience that there is no good applying to Heaven for earthly comfort. Heaven can give heavenly comfort; no other kind. And earth cannot give earthly comfort either. . . . There is no earthly comfort in the long run." The four steps will take us as far as we can get, and, in any case, will insulate us from the worst illusions and travesties of what used to be called on television, "Love, American Style."

The occupational hazard for any authors thus assuming something of a prophetic stance is spurious certainty and self-righteousness. We have tried very hard to avoid this pitfall. It has proven difficult to write a book on love because the challenges of love, romantic or other, remain constantly to confront (and sometimes to stymie) the authors, who could never get what scholars like to call "an authoritative perspective" on the subject. Archimedes said he could move the world with his wonderful lever if he could but find a place outside the world to stand. Similarly for us, we could perhaps have more to say about love, and say it more "authoritatively," if we only had what no human being can ever have—an angel's view of the world. In the absence of this advantage, we can only offer our thoughts and advice with humility and hope.

*C. S. Lewis, *The Four Loves* (New York: Harcourt Brace Jovanovich, Inc., 1960), p. 190.

ACKNOWLEDGMENTS

As with our first book, *For the Love of Children,* this book has turned out to be a collaboration in the fullest sense of the word. Both of us, working together, found our ideas meshing and developing beyond what either of us alone might have reached.

Ed's long exposure to the creative thinking of his colleague and friend, Dr. William Glasser, creator of Reality Therapy, is reflected in many of the ideas found in this book. The phrase "Reality Therapy" may not occur, but the spirit of that wonderfully effective method is rarely absent.

Both of us wish to thank our devoted typist-reader, Frances Rehm, and to acknowledge with gratitude the decisive contribution of Jack Miles.

Edward E. Ford
Steven Englund

Scottsdale, Arizona

CONTENTS

INTRODUCTION:

Toward a
More Permanent Love

Perhaps the strongest, most definitive drive of the human species is the drive toward love. It may also be the most multifaceted, the most talked- and written-about, and the least understood or fulfilled. Water, water everywhere, and not a drop to drink, runs the old saw, and the same could be said for love. We live in a society that chokes from overuse of the word *love*. We hear it applied to every situation, from the most primitive instinctual urges ("I love apple pie." "He made love to the call girl.") to the crassest excesses of commercial advertising in a society gone mad on consumerism ("Love" bath and beauty products; Chevrolet's "Luv" truck). Yet the possibility of even understanding what love is, let alone of

1

practicing it enduringly, seems steadily to recede from our collective grasp. In place of love we have concocted many culturally hallowed substitutes—caricatures, placebos, distortions. But the measure of our desperation in clinging to them is the measure of their fundamental insufficiency and our dissatisfaction.

I am a father, a husband, a friend, a counselor, and a therapist. In my private and public lives, I am called upon to deal in—to earn and to spend—the love currency all day long. I am fifty-two years old, and it has taken me the greater part of that half century to fight my way clear of the external and internal forces silently prodding me to seek and worship the love substitutes. People come to me every day—both friends and clients—voicing what seems at first glance to be a confusing myriad of problems: "We don't enjoy going out anymore"; "Our sex life isn't what it used to be"; "All we do are the same old things together"; "I can't seem to find anyone who loves me"; "I'm getting tired of the singles or couples or gay bars"; "Marriage is a bore." Gradually I have come to realize that such complaints and laments are not problems but symptoms, symptoms of an underlying sociocultural weakness now so common as to be perhaps the issue of our time: the need to learn how to love.

As the motivations of survival and scarcity have given way in our history to those of security and affluence, virtually every aspect of human life has been affected. For a long time we congratulated ourselves on the boons of our industrial civilization; now (in fact for the past decade or more) we have been obliged to fill up the liability column of the ledger. The wonderland of enlarged capacities and acquisitions has been offset by a corresponding set of awesome risks and drawbacks. Affluence may have vanquished the psychology and economy

2

of scarcity, but the victory has brought us the curse of wanton materialism, not to mention pollution, the energy crisis, overpopulation, declining education and health standards, rising crime, drug addiction, and more.

Freedom from survival needs has permitted us the unprecedented luxury of unbounded self-consciousness and self-concern, which has, over the past quarter century, burgeoned into a maze of centers, institutions, therapies, techniques, psychologies, and practices intended to explore, expand, and develop the individual self and its capabilities. But the paradoxical result seems stubbornly to be a steady weakening and diminishment of the self—of its executor, the will; its spirituality, the soul; its corporeality, the body; and its capacity for relationships, the art of loving.

Perhaps this result was to have been expected from so self-interested a quest. Long before Alex Haley's *Roots*, Simone Weil, the French philosopher, signaled mankind's fundamental need for rootedness in community. In the absence of community, very likely no amount of strenuous individual effort can supply what the group gave with natural and unconscious ease. As with so many other things worth having in life, apparently a healthy, rooted love relationship can be achieved only as a by-product of a larger process that does not focus on the relationship directly. (How many doors, we find, open only after we have stopped pounding on them.)

In the area of what has come to be called "interpersonal relations," therefore, times have changed for the better and for the worse, but mainly for the worse. Where economic scarcity obliged us to work together, the arrival of security has left us unsuccessfully working *at being together*. Many of the most glorious achievements of the consumer economy—the automobile, the television set, the computer, the fantastic

3

array of audiovisual technology—have extensively eroded our ability to converse meaningfully in groups. And the "science of communications" and the pervasiveness of the media have not managed to repair the damage. They have, on the contrary, contributed to it by perfecting the systems of transmission of words while neglecting the people transmitting the message as well as the content of what is being transmitted.

Turning to the art of loving itself, we confront an interesting set of developments. On the one hand, the range of what psychologists call object choices—whom to love, whom not to love—has been immeasurably expanded so that we of the twentieth century are able to fuss and fidget over the question of who is the recipient of our romantic love to a far, far greater degree than people of any other historical era. For it is useful to recall that during most of the three thousand years of Western civilization, human beings did not choose their spouses; instead we learned to love the person whom fate and socioeconomic forces threw out to be our conjugal mate. Moreover, even in the considerably loosened constraints of contemporary society, we still do not literally choose ninety percent of the objects of our loving—for example, parents, relatives, children, God.[1]

On the other hand, as is so often the case in human history, the seeming expansion of social freedom has led to a greater, subtler form of psychological restricition, even enslavement. Significant increases in a person's capacity to choose romantic love objects are only good and advantageous if he or she has the maturity and strength of mind—in a word, the will—to make rational, progressive use of the freedom. In the absence of strong will, freedom risks becoming mere license. And that, sadly, is what has happened to us. The strengthening of the individual will has not taken place. On the contrary, for a wide variety of reasons—from the loosening of traditional social constraints to misguided forms of state intervention in people's lives to the consumer psychology and culture created by Madison Avenue through the media—the very concept of individual responsibility, autonomy, and potency has been disparaged and ignored.[2]

In these circumstances, the enlarged range of object choice in romantic loving has become a poison, not an antidote. Choice has become caprice; it has become the *carte blanche* of our emotions, appetites, and psychological fantasy. In the absence of strong and wise will, enlarged choice has only permitted romantic love to become manipulative, fickle, victimizing, emotionalized, and freedom-reducing. Caprice and license have given Eros (romantic love) the ability to monopolize our love energy and, thereby, Eros, itself infected, infects all the rest of loving as well. The unending parade of unhappy worshippers of romantic love who wend their way into consulting rooms, encounter groups, and law courts around the nation is the living proof of the abject failure of our version (or vision) of romantic love to create healthy, lasting relationships. Most people show no inclination toward understanding or changing their mode of loving, and the consequence is the rapidly increasing number of divorces, separations, and short-lived romantic relationships.

This is not the worst of it, however, for the impermanence, emotionalism, and self-centeredness of our kind of romantic love are distorting and infecting our practice of *all* love. Beyond the obvious mess it has made of its own dominion, romantic love brings harm and pain elsewhere. Our reduced willingness to cope with stress or undertake self-sacrifice in love has led us to push our aging parents and relatives to the margins of our collective and individual lives. We indulge our children, coddle and overstimulate them emotionally, yet do not spend enough time with them,[3] and, worst of all, we eagerly educate them in the worship of romantic love as we have been educated. We either ignore God and religion entirely, or, worse, since in many cases the absence of belief may be an honest, even religious stance, we fling ourselves into romanticized, emotionalized religious movements that tend to distort the meaning and weaken the strength of our love for God.

Our concept of romantic love has, furthermore, led us to distort our images of the opposite sex, seen particularly in the masculine view of women as emotional-sexual objects or domesticated helpers. And finally, even the realm of friendship has been marred by an eroticized society which presumes that all profound and intense friendships harbor sexual intent. Even when this is not the case, friendship is thought trivial (decidedly inferior to Eros) or made altogether impossible (particularly among many unmarried, middle-aged women) because of the stifling competition for sexual mates.

In short, the problem of romantic love has become the problem of love. The transiency, fantasy, and narcissism that mark our romantic loving have shown up in most other major organs of "love's body." Contrary to what we have been told and have come to expect, there are no quick or easy remedies for this ailment. Indeed, abandoning the expectation of cures is the first step to take on the path to recovery. But it is only the first. Beyond that, we must struggle to resurrect the ancient tie between romantic love and all loving and between all loving and the will. This means we must sever the overlarge connection between romantic love and the emotions and appetites. Eros has become for us a game of fantasy, feelings, sexual gratification, and self-centered manipulation; for romantic love to be healthy and permanent, it must be returned to its position in the larger constellation of love and will.

I have no doubt that this relocation, or restoration, of romantic love to its rightful position is possible. But I am also certain that it is difficult. Erich Fromm noted over twenty years ago how hard it is to love authentically in a society and culture organized along nonloving, even counterloving, lines. Nothing that has come to pass in the interim gives me cause to disagree with Fromm that "People capable of love, under the present system, are necessarily the exceptions; love is by necessity a marginal phenomenon in present-day Western society."[4] Nonetheless, the capability does exist, and not simply in "the exceptions" but in *all* of us, who, though we fail at loving much (even most) of the time, occasionally express love, erotic or other, as it should be expressed. Even in a culture that is enchanted by romantic love and basks (or writhes) on a bed of mercurial emotions, love-as-usual attends to its unsung business as best it can. In observing its quiet expression in various moments in the relationships we maintain with our parents, our children, our close friends, our God—as hard as these relationships may be to maintain and as poorly as many of us handle them—we will detect in our loving the telltale traces of care, responsibility, knowledge, respect, selflessness, transcendence, and joy—all of which insure that such loving is an act of will. We can thus learn something of value for the redefinition and reconstruction of romantic love in our time.

Beyond the few precious moments of our own authentic experiences of loving, there is also the example of the past—of our parents, our ancestors, and the great thinkers of

7

history—to call upon. Finally, I shall be presenting some very practical steps in the course of this book, which, if followed, may lead you (puffing and sweating) along the path toward permanent love. So be of good cheer. Cynical resignation is out of place; only hope and lots of concentrated effort are in order from now on.

* * *

Before taking another step, I should tell what I mean by love; but in so doing I also have to say that I don't think abstractions, generalizations, and definitions of love are mainly what we need. Whole sections of libraries house essays, treatises, discourses—all manner of fictional and nonfictional works—that treat love. To say something new is therefore both impossible and undesirable; straining for novelty on a matter so basic would only add to our delay in finding love by haggling over the definition of it. As a French playwright wrote, "There is no such thing as love; there is only evidence of love." Nonetheless, because my own education impels me to this sort of thing and because I think it highly desirable that we as a civilization do not lose touch with the wisdom of our collective past, I shall adduce some of my favorite long-standing descriptions and definitions of love from the great minds of the Western world.

> *Love is all we have, the only way that each can help the other.*
>
> Euripides, *Orestes*

8

It is love, not reason, that is stronger than death.
   Thomas Mann, *Death in Venice*

Love consists in this, that two solitudes protect
and border and salute each other.
   Rainer Maria Rilke, *Letters to a Young Poet*

Love, whether sexual, parental, or fraternal, is
essentially sacrificial, and prompts a man to give
his life for his friends.
   George Santayana, *The Life of Reason*

One cannot be strong without love. For love is
not an irrelevant emotion; it is the blood of life,
the power of reunion of the separated.
   Paul Tillich, *The Eternal Now*

Though I speak with the tongues of men and of
angels, and have not Love, I am become as
sounding brass, or a tinkling cymbal.
   And though I have the gift of prophecy, and
understand all mysteries, and all knowledge; and
though I have all faith, so that I could move
mountains, and have not love, I am nothing.
   And though I bestow all my goods to feed the
poor, and though I give my body to be burned,
and have not Love, it profits me nothing.
   Love is patient and kind; Love is not jealous, or
conceited, or proud; Love is not ill-mannered, or
selfish, or irritable; Love does not keep a record of
wrongs; Love is not happy with evil, but rejoices

9

with truth. Love bears with all things, believes all
things, hopes all things, endures all things.
    So there abide, Faith, Hope, Love, these three.
But the greatest of these is Love.

I Corinthians 13

As children of the Western tradition, perhaps simply as human beings, we all know what love is. It doesn't require high-falutin language to express itself. Simply, love is the willingness to work at getting along with another. It is the willingness to find the self by losing it in another; it's the capacity to give to, and to work with, another human being when you're discouraged, lazy, self-pitying, depressed; it's the willingness to risk rejection and humiliation for the sake of building a relationship; it's the effort needed to climb out of one's personal wishes, needs, hopes, and consider those of another person. Love is self-transcendence, literally the only chance we mortals have of partially escaping from the prisons of our aloneness and selfhood by taking the risk of sharing in a newer, larger identity with another person. And for many people, human love is ultimately the reflection of divine love, which is the source and meaning of life; and for them to *work* at human love is to *understand* divine love better, just as the action of divine love is what empowers human love and makes it possible.

This is a book, then, about learning how to love and to construct enduring relationships built on love. There are many kinds of love, as writers from St. Paul to C. S. Lewis and Erich Fromm have reminded us; but I think most people would agree that at the heart of the matter, sexual, fraternal, parental, and spiritual love are all manifestations of a single underlying human (and divine) capacity. Nonetheless, without wanting to quibble over this, I think most people first experience the fullness of the love phenomenon in its romantic-sexual incarnation. Even if they then go on to embrace further, equally intense and demanding forms of love (parental, humanitarian, spiritual), the fact remains that the construction and maintenance of the romantic tie continues to be a, if not the, primordial requirement and challenge of their emotional lives. Therefore, because my own experience has followed this common scenario, and because this book is written for a wide audience, I should say at the outset that I shall be speaking about love most often in the context of a romantic-sexual relationship—the love that binds lovers. But it is important that the two lovers be married. It is not my job as a therapist to raise moral objections to an unmarried couple's living together. But precisely as a therapist, I must point out that if a couple are just living together because they doubt that they have what it takes for the long haul, then in the end they won't have what it takes for the long haul. That doubt in them will become a self-fulfilling prophecy. Sometimes a couple will feel that they are not ready for marriage. They want to test their relationship and try to build up strength within it; or they want to build up their separate strengths for the relationship. Most often, this doesn't work. If the necessary strength is lacking, just living together will not provide it. As we shall see in a moment, the partners probably need to develop their strength, their confidence, in other ways and only then try to make a go of their lives together.

New York theater critic Joanna Kyd published an article not long ago in the New York Times (May 28, 1978) entitled "Unmarriage." Ms. Kyd is divorced, and in the company of a divorced man, she had spent an evening in the apartment of an unmarried couple who were living together. The evening began well but ended awkwardly, sadly.

I said my good-nights and walked the dark streets back to my neighborhood. I'll never forget how lost those people seemed. How lost I felt. These are real unmarried people. Marriages don't seem to work anymore, but there's a new lost generation that grows bigger every day. Because the truth is that unmarriage doesn't work either.

I have seen demonstrated again and again the truth that unmarriage doesn't work any better than marriage, and often doesn't work as well.

Unless I am willing to promise you that I will stick around long enough for you and me to work on and grow in our capacity to love each other, then we will never actually grow. If each of us has to be ready to pack up at any time because our relationship is just one of mutual convenience, then we will never know the stress and tension of long-term compromise. Is compromise a triumph or a defeat? I call it a triumph. Not the kind of triumph that is won on the battlefield by a general, but the kind that is achieved by an artist.

Marriage vows, when you come down to it, represent *a commitment to working for permanent love by making compromises*. True, the large number of failed marriages proves that there is nothing automatic about the vows; but properly understood and respected, these vows can release a kind of power in the marriage partners—a strong, urgent desire to make the commitment work. Couples who are living together without the benefit of vows are almost always doing so *because the relationship can more easily be broken that way*. Small wonder then if relationships that are designed to be easily broken are frequently broken. Rather than struggle through the compromises that would make permanent love possible, such couples simply call the relationship off. I have seen this again and again in my counseling practice, and I wonder: If my own wife and I had been just living together during the early years of our marriage, would we be living together now?

To regard loving as an art to be practiced is a lyrical, captivating approach. Erich Fromm's book *The Art of Loving* has justifiably won the acclaim of millions. Few people have written more perceptively than he on the high theory of this art. On the other hand, as characterizes many great theoreticians, he has not taken the same pains and time to construct a *practice* of loving.

Fromm writes discerningly of the discipline, patience, and concentration required for the practice of any art; and then he analyzes at length the need for "the *overcoming* of one's *narcissism*," for "objectivity," for the use of the "faculty of reason," for "the necessary condition of rational *faith*" and the "productiveness" that underlies it, for "courage" in the existential sense; and he writes of the inhibitions and obstructions to loving that arise within capitalist society. How, in practice, does a person achieve the "overcoming of narcissism" in his relationship with his lover? How does he learn to observe, criticize, and detach himself from the uncongenialities of contemporary society that undermine true loving? How does he employ the "faculty of reason" when he is hip-deep in raw emotion? Or how does he link faith and courage with impotence, excessive dependence on sex, or the routinization of his conjugal life? Fromm did not raise, let alone answer, these questions—nor am I faulting him for not doing so.

If, however, you deal every day with confused human

13

beings suffering from the pain of not loving or of poor and inadequate loving, then you are obliged to beg, borrow, steal, or invent a means—*a practice*—that will help them to help themselves. I am nothing more than a working counselor and therapist who spends his professional life working with troubled people. My concerns focus entirely on helping them (and myself) to love more truly, more fulfillingly, more lastingly; and the experience that gives me the confidence to write a book about loving is taken, not from the theory I have read or (even less) created, but from the day-in/day-out techniques (bag of tricks, if you will) I have been obliged to devise and collect in order to help people. This is what this book is about; the success I have had with my techniques is its single justification.

In view of what I have just written, it is perhaps mildly paradoxical that Erich Fromm provides the transition to this presentation of my own practical method of creating artists of loving. Two lines from his book stuck in my brain when I first read them over a decade ago: "The practice of faith and courage begins with *the small details of daily life* [my emphasis]"; and "One attitude, indispensable for the practice of the art of loving, . . . is basic for the practice of love: *activity* [my emphasis]."[5] Fromm never developed these thoughts along the lines in which I later came to understand them, but they unconsciously signalled to me the general direction a practical methodology of loving should take. Life is the sum of its thousand daily parts, of those countless unobserved little actions that determine with almost ironclad inflexibility the direction and quality of our existence and hence the direction and quality of our loving. When all the "peak experiences" have shone for their brief (and important) moments, and after the embraces and passionate promises have been exchanged,

14

the nature and course of love inevitably returns to being determined by the subtle unfolding of the patterns of daily living.

The activity of which Fromm spoke was the "inner activity of love" in the heart of the individual person. But the activity, or activities, that actually determine an individual person's capability for love, as well as determining the actual character (the strength or weakness) of his love relationships with real people, are the *outer* activities—the behavior patterns and patterns of interaction—which he shares with those people, or which he performs alone, throughout the days of his life. The "inner activity of love" is not a practical concept that is useful in the therapeutic encounter. But external activity, or behavior, is very definitely a reality that we, counselor and client, can examine and change; and I have found that a person's "inner" feelings, capacities, and understandings will change and grow *according to changes in his behavior.*

Whatever may be true about the art of loving as an abstract formulation, when you come right down to building permanent love relationships between people, the single most decisive factor is the quantity and quality of the activity they share in their daily lives. So don't tell me about your marriage vows or even your sexual compatibility; don't tell me about how often you have "deep talks" about your relationship or how you feel about each other or how much money you spend on vacations and passive entertainment. Tell me about what you did last night, or yesterday morning, or last Saturday noon, or the previous Thursday evening, or the Monday before that. Tell me about all the long, flat plateaus and plains that lie between the peak experiences of sex, vacations, and heart-to-heart talks.

In all events, whether I am theoretically right or wrong in my practical outlook, there flowed from these insights a kind of pragmatic sequence, a series of steps or stages, which again and again I found worked as a way of leading people to build stronger, more fulfilling and enduring love relationships. These steps are the subject matter of this book. They are not complex or esoteric, nor are they intended to contribute to the theory of love. I offer them only as one tried-and-tested means of helping people to do their loving more fruitfully.

There is no easy way to love, and even less, to build "permanent" love. Indeed the two terms, *permanence* and *love*, seem mutually exclusive in our society—a fact that becomes dramatically clear when we consult the separation and divorce statistics or simply note the frequency with which love relationships are collapsing like tenpins around us. We are not the society of our forebears, who clung to endurance. For the better, we have discovered individualism, human potential, self-expression, and liberation; and for the worse, we have encountered their darker sides: impatience, transience, narcissism, self-indulgence, brittleness of emotions.

In our rush to explore and expand our sacred selves, and in our near-total dependency upon technological and psychological labor-saving devices, we have lost touch with the benevolent, the altruistic impulse of love, as well as the degree of effort that love requires. In a society that idolizes youth, doubts tradition, rewards the ingenuity of avoidance, and expects immediate sensual gratification, a sense of the permanent is lost. The willingness to build, to suffer, to lose, and to start again—qualities that our forefathers were obliged to develop in their world of scarcity and survival—are traits we only dimly understand, let alone value and possess. But love demands these things; and as the pain of frustrated love and pseudolove mounts, we are at last reduced to a position of openness to rediscovering these lost qualities. I hope this book can play a small, helping role in our rediscovery.

The steps I shall be proposing are not an "easy way" to anything; they are simply a structured and practical way of showing us where we went wrong and how we could go right. And they make certain presuppositions. First of all, they presuppose a partner who is similarly committed to the same basic sort of love relationship that you are. Fundamentally, love is love is love; in the last analysis, it is a unified capacity—but only in the last analysis. All along the way there are varieties of love, and it won't do to follow these steps (or any steps) if you are committed to a close friendship whereas your partner yearns for a romance. Nor, for that matter, will it suffice if one of you is committed ninety percent and the other only ten percent to maintaining the relationship. There will be rhythms of effort, of course, and one partner's time of harvest may be his lover's time to sow; or indeed, (as often happens in crisis) each may be making heavy demands that the other momentarily cannot fulfill. This is not what I'm getting at when I talk of the need for equal commitment between you. I mean only that in the long haul, very, very few people (I have been blessed to know a handful) are gifted by God with the capacity for endless, unrewarded giving in a love relationship. At some point, the giver begins to accumulate an ever-growing reservoir of resentment toward the taker. That reservoir may be a subterranean lake, but eventually it will break through all dams and defenses and destroy any chance for permanence. Thus I insist on some basic equality of concern, of mutuality, in the couples I try to help.

If the first presupposition is equality of commitment, the

17

second is shared priorities. You and your partner must agree about where you rank your relationship among the many goals that you are pursuing. Is it more important or less important than a successful career? More important or less important than beauty? More important or less important than popularity? If one of you is involved in politics, are politics more important or less important than your relationship? If one of you plays golf or owns a boat or belongs to a club or has a dear but intrusive friend (or family), are any of these things more important than your relationship with your lover? Only you can answer; but it is important that you and your lover answer in the same way. It may be that for each of you, a career is more important than the relationship. So long as you both feel that way, your expectations of the relationship will be realistic, but your relationship, in my opinion, will eventually be in trouble. I believe that if a relationship is to be permanent, it has to rank first on the priority list. Even on little things. A close friend recently lost his wife, and he was relating to me how he had to be constantly attentive to his love for his wife. "I would come home from work and reach for the newspaper. Glancing over my paper, I would see her there at the stove," he said. "My God, is the evening paper more important than my wife? Later on in the evening she might say, 'I would be pleased if you would take a walk with me,' and I would respond, 'I'm a little tired, honey, and besides, I played racquetball today, so I've gotten my exercise.' Again, where were my priorities? They were so easily misplaced, especially in little things."

After equality of commitment and shared priorities, the third presupposition is that you have reasonable strength in your own personality. As we shall shortly see, the second of my four steps is "What You Can Do on Your Own" for your

18

relationship. But I want to say right now *that you won't be able to do anything on your own for your relationship unless you have been able, over a period of time, to do a few things on your own for yourself*. You have to have your own act pretty well together before you can team up with another performer. So much in a relationship depends on your own self-confidence. When difficulties come along, you have to believe that you *can* work them out. And how do you gain confidence in your ability to work them out? You gain it from the confidence you have gained earlier in trying and succeeding in other endeavors. You need a reservoir of strengthening activities to protect you from slipping into destructive self-criticism. Analyzing your behavior is one thing. Giving up on yourself, ceasing to believe that you can take charge of your own life, is quite another. The list of possible human endeavors is endless. The major source of strength (other than love) comes from what we do, our work life. From this activity comes status, recognition, and a sense of responsibility, all of which fulfill one of our basic human needs, the need for worth. There are other avenues of strength, however, and just to simplify, I have chosen five of them. The more stength you can develop in each of them, the better off you will be in making your relationship last. In a sense, they will be a resource from which you can constantly draw.

(1) *Service to others*. Ours is increasingly a service-oriented economy. Many, perhaps most, of us who are "gainfully employed," as the saying goes, are giving some kind of service. Teachers serve their students. Mechanics serve motorists in service (!) stations. Anyone involved in commerce is faced every day with others who need his or her service. And then there is the service provided in that most important of all "service stations," the home. Mothers,

fathers, and grown or nearly-grown children living at home—each is in a position to provide service of some sort. Indeed, none quite escapes providing service even if he or she would like to. The question is: how good at it are you? If cooking is your service, do you try to cook well? Have you learned to take pleasure in putting a good meal on the table? And then, apart from either home or work, there are the service challenges of church, community, and the world as a whole. Do you ever volunteer for church or civic work? Try it; there can be a secret dividend. You can gain confidence in your ability to provide service, and that confidence can eventually be a huge help in making a relationship last.

(2) *Creativity*. Can you make something from nothing, or at least from nothing more than raw materials? Can you make a dress from a bolt of cloth? A table from a piece of unfinished lumber? Delicious vegetables or beautiful flowers from earth, water, sunshine, and a few seeds? Can you make music in a choir or glee club or from a piano? A poem from a piece of blank paper and your dreams? You may well have tried one or more of these activities. Think of other possibilities until you find something you can do or have done, because the experience of creating is a crucial one for us. Unlike God, human beings do not create from nothing; but at times, they seem to come close. What lay before Beethoven but blank paper and the memory of what the instruments of an orchestra sounded like? And yet from that emptiness came the strains of the Ninth Symphony and other works that have lifted the human heart for hundreds of years. We are never more godlike than when we try to make something from nothing, however humble our work may seem. And here, too, there is a dividend for permanent love. Making a marriage work is like making something from nothing. In place of the unfinished

lumber or the uncut cloth, substitute the unshared lives of two single people. Making them fit together well like sleeves onto a coat or legs onto a table calls for patience and care and accuracy. It calls, in a word, for creativity. If you have confidence in your creativity because of your success in small tasks, you will have confidence in your creativity with this big one.

(3) *Physical exercise*. You may smile that I include something as humble as exercise on the same list with something as exalted as creativity, but that's what the human being is, a blend of the humble and the exalted. What does exercise give you? Well, obviously enough, it gives you strength—not just a sense of strength, but *real* strength. Take running, for example. The first day you start, you come home red-faced and puffing after just one block. But the second day, you run two blocks and come home a little less red-faced, puffing a little less hard. You can feel the strength flowing little by little into your lungs and your legs. Now, strength in the legs does not automatically become strength in the personality, but it can help. You don't have to achieve championship levels. In fact, you can even be physically handicapped. What counts is that you set out to do something with your body—something that costs you effort, that hurts a little—and then just do it!

(4) *Social life*. I'm not thinking narrowly of the dating that single people do or the entertaining that couples do. I'm not excluding those, but my terms are a little broader. Calling a friend on the telephone is a part of social life. So is writing a letter, going out to eat, or taking a walk with a friend of either sex. More formal gatherings like voters' groups or recreational classes or sports clubs certainly count as well. In brief, everything that involves doing something with others,

21

especially when conversation is involved, is social life. And here the dividend—you've guessed it already—is learning how to talk![6] We all learned how to talk when we were two years old or so, but there are differing levels of ability and differing levels of acquired skill. Some people have "the gift of gab" and have had it since the first word bubbled up from their baby throats. Others are more slow-spoken or even awkward in speech. But as in exercise or creativity, everyone has a little something to work with. How many times have we heard it said of a marriage that "communications broke down"? There were those long, painful, or just empty silences. Nothing to say; or so very much to say but no way to begin saying it. If you're going to make a relationship last, you're going to have to be prepared to break those silences.

(5) *Intellectual life*. Ignorance, the saying goes, is a curable disease, and one of the major cures for it is reading. No one, no matter how full his or her life, can live more than one lifetime. Even a long life is no more than what the poet A. E. Housman called a "little room." But through reading, you can participate in lives from all times and all places as you enter into them through the printed page. So often we believe that we are not as interesting as the people we read about in magazines or see on television. We find ourselves, in Shakespeare's phrase, "desiring this man's art and that man's scope." But the remedy for this particular lack of confidence is at hand. Another poet, Emily Dickinson, described the remedy well in a famous quatrain:

I never saw a Moor—
I never saw the Sea—
Yet know I how the Heather looks
And what a wave must be.

22

She, who scarcely left the little town of Amherst during her whole life, knew heather and moors from reading and thinking and learning. The "jet set" may travel the world and never see it. Less travel and more thought may well produce a more genuinely interesting mind in the long run. The philosopher Immanuel Kant, who lived his entire life in the small town of Koenigsberg, amazed his English visitors with his knowledge of London. So wide was his reading and so great his pleasure in maps that he knew the very streets of London better than they did. In reading and in schooling, in writing and in the discussing of what has been read, the most ordinary person may little by little become company fit for princes and poets. When contemplating a long-lasting, permanent relationship, do you fear that you will bore your partner? One way to strengthen your confidence is to mingle, through the potent magic of the printed word, with the wonderful human beings of the past. In troubled times, they can be powerful allies.

* * *

I have spoken of three presuppositions for permanent love:
(1) equal commitment,
(2) shared priorities,
(3) reasonable strength of personality.
Of these three, I have spent by far the longest time speaking of the third. By now, if you are like many people I have counseled, you are rather anxiously examining your own personality for signs of strength: "What am I doing now? How's my creativity? My social life? My intellectual life?" And so on. Please relax. Remember, I said *reasonable* strength. Building a lasting relationship is not like running the four-minute mile or scaling Mount Everest. Sure, there are

thousands of divorces each year, but there are also thousands of marriages that make it. Though a lasting love is a wonderful thing, it is, in the end, a very ordinary thing. Think of how many ordinary people have done it! Are you less capable of it than they are? Frankly, if you have been patient enough to read even this far, then chances are pretty good that you do have what it takes. Meanwhile, as you work to improve your chances, remember that an atmosphere of extreme criticism, whether it is self-criticism or criticism from another, is not conducive to growth. Love and confidence—including self-love and self-confidence—grow best through gentleness and patience. In the Bible, God is described as "slow to anger and of great kindness." We need not be harder on ourselves than God is.

In the last analysis, human beings are held to one another by ten thousand ties, only a few of which may be rational and articulable. We rarely select even our friends on the basis of a rational evaluation of their qualities; and God knows we don't select our children or our parents on that basis.

We are perhaps least rational in our selection of a lover. But if it were otherwise, if we were paired off scientifically, like stud horses and brood mares in some giant controlled breeding experiment, then a book such as mine (or the thousands of others about marriage, love, or relationships) would be unnecessary. But we neither love nor live by reason alone. Reason is only one ingredient in our stew. The challenge of permanent love, therefore, is to create itself in a less-than-rational, imperfect situation; to grow up between lovers who came together not for all the "right" reasons, but for the usual, common reasons. The perfect relationship, like the perfect man or the perfect woman, lies beyond our grasp. Enduring love, however, precisely because it does not presuppose perfection, is within our grasp. It is a beautiful

flower, but it is not all that delicate. It can have the tenacity
of a weed, refusing to die even in the ongoing, stress-filled,
imperfect world of men and women. I have never been able
(nor would I want) to get out of that world, and I humbly offer
this book as one traveler's guide to his fellows.

NOTES:

[1]Historically, only friendship has always entailed an element of
choice. Yet as a matter of practical fact, many, if not most, of our
closest cronies, colleagues, and pals are people whom we really
didn't select but learned to care for because of circumstances.
Nonetheless, the greater degree of choice in the love that is
friendship has often led people understandably to view friendship as
a much needed vacation from the "obligatory" love of family or
social relationships.

[2]Just one crucial example serves to buttress this point. Medicine, in
collaboration with contemporary psychology and the social sciences,
has provided all sorts of categories—notably the classifications of
mental or emotional illness, the notion of social deviance and
pathology, character disorders, and so on—which entirely undercut
the role of choice, responsibility, and duty on the part of an
individual while at the same time encouraging his childlike
dependence on experts. The treatment of most physical and mental
problems in our society utterly reduces the patient to creature status
and the doctors (M.D.s and Ph.D.s) to minigods of adjustment and
rehabilitation. Largely unneeded, even dangerous, programs of
treatment involving chemicals, surgical interventions, shock
therapy, behavioral modification, and so on, entirely undermine the
concept, let alone the practice, of will.

[3]Edward E. Ford and Steven Englund, *For the Love of Children*
(Garden City, N.Y.: Doubleday, 1977), chaps. 1 and 3.

[4]Erich Fromm, *The Art of Loving: An Enquiry into the Nature of Love*
(New York: Harper & Row, 1956), p. 111.

[5]Fromm, *The Art of Loving*, p. 107.

[6]Edward E. Ford, *Why Marriage?* (Niles, Ill.: Argus
Communications, 1974), chap. 10.

25

STEP ONE:

What a Couple Can Do Together

Human relationships, especially romantic ones, are generators of feelings. In fair weather, this fact is usually not problematic because the feelings generated are largely positive and often euphoric. The patterns of behavior, the day-to-day interactions of a thousand and one varieties, that create these "good feelings" go largely unobserved by the participants of a relationship, who have no reason to be aware of them.

Comes the rain, and emotions can change with the swiftness of a falling barometer. In an instant, clear skies become overcast, and a monsoon of negative feelings—anger, hurt, insecurity, disappointment, disillusionment, loneliness—sweeps over us in torrents. Suddenly the question of where these feelings originated takes on importance and urgency. Ironically, however, the very intensity and multiplicity of the feelings prevent our seeing beyond them into the core of personal behavior and interaction with other people that gave rise to them. At precisely the time when we need maximum clarity of vision and understanding in order to deal with feelings, these very feelings permit us no detachment or peace—no opportunity to employ calm reason or exercise will.

This circumstance is a pity, but commonplace and entirely comprehensible, as innate to the human condition as any of the conflicts arising from the fact that we are physical, rational, emotional, and spiritual beings whose four systems do not always mesh like the silent harmony of a costly Swiss watch. The almost irresistible urge for anyone caught up in bad feelings is to deal with them (or try to) by identifying and analyzing them. Even for the experienced therapist, there is a strong temptation to come to grips directly with the client's negative emotions in order to afford some instant relief by resolving the immediate, *apparent* problem.

Sometimes such action on the client's or the therapist's part is unavoidable. Sometimes feelings are so overwhelming they may not be ignored with impunity. But usually I find they can be; at the very least, they may be pushed aside sooner than most people (clients and therapists) are willing to do. I'm not a cruel man or a cold therapist, but I find that a brisk, almost-but-not-quite impatient attitude toward emotions is, in the last analysis, the most effective, least cruel way of helping people come in out of the raging storm of bad feelings. For example, I might say, "I can see you are really upset. Well, you're in the right place. I work with upset people, even

28

people as upset as you." They then don't have to be as upset as they were. They have my attention, and they have made their point. Talking about feelings affords, at best, only momentary relief, and often it does so at the long-run expense of keeping the client's and the therapist's attention off the key issue.

And what is that? *Behavior—what people do, alone and together.* Very early on in the first counseling session, therefore, I ask a couple the question, "In as much detail as you can provide, would you please tell me how you live your lives? What do you actually do alone together in the course of an average day and an average week?" The question is simple enough, but I have to wield it like a jackhammer to blast my way through the hard granite of their urge to talk about bad feelings. They'll throw out a few unconsidered generalities about their lives together and then dive right back into the caldron of churning emotions. When this happens again and again, I reformulate the question and put it this way: "When was the last time the two of you did something enjoyable alone together? What did you do?" The longer the silence before they answer, the greater my concern for the marriage.

Questions like these are crucial to discerning the strengths and weaknesses of a relationship, but most people do not understand why. They are irritated by the seeming triviality of my wish to know all the detail of their daily interaction. They are certain that I am missing the "big issues." What I can never get them to see—until afterward—is that the exact opposite is true: what they regard as trivial is causal and decisive; what they are overwhelmed by and obsessed with is transient, ungraspable, and derivative. Their answers invariably reflect the same dilemma: the sheer amount of tandem behavior—of doing *anything* together—is minimal in a troubled relationship. The amount of positive, strength-building behavior (and we'll begin to define this in a moment) is virtually nonexistent. For unhappy lovers, therefore, recalling occasions of mutually satisfying interaction is hard; the examples they offer are paltry, uncertain, or sometimes altogether impossible to arrive at. If the effort of finding these examples dissolves into further fighting and a rawer display of emotions, then I have to separate the couple and recommence the questioning with each person separately. And this occasionally happens.

Eventually, however, the truth emerges. The troubles, problems, bad feelings in the relationship are a consequence of the lack of meaningful, satisfying, positive interaction. The pair isn't doing much alone together; and what they are doing isn't very strength-creating or fulfilling to their individual lives or to their life as a couple. The old insight proves true: behavior creates feelings; if you wish to change the feelings, you'll first have to change the behavior.

What constitutes behavior that is not strengthening to a relationship? Well, to be truthful, just about all the interaction many couples engage in during the few moments they are awake together in the morning plus the time in late afternoon when one or both return home from their jobs, exchange routine greetings, share the evening meal in front of the television, and discuss the standard banalities about job, children, and household, to the time that they offer one another the perfunctory good-night kiss. Have I been unfair in my portrait? Have I purposely set up a straw couple? Well, then, let's paint a different picture. The couple greet each other with a passionate embrace, get giddy over cocktails, go out to dinner and a movie, and make rip-roaring love before they pass out for the night in each other's arms. Is the mutual interaction necessarily more relationship-enhancing in the latter instance than in the former? Is the latter couple— still in the euphoric weeks of being newlyweds—automatically building up for their marriage the sort of strength that will see them through the unavoidable stress of two lives lived as one? Are the all-American, hallowed activities of television, cocktails, dining out, movies, and sex providing the substance from which permanent love can concoct a satisfying meal? No.

Nonstrengthening behavior is any behavior that provides short-run stimulus *without providing long-term growth.* It provides a quick way to achieve temporary good feelings by short-circuiting, or bypassing, the normal, time-sanctioned means of generating lasting good feelings. In that sense, behavior that does not build relational confidence or strength is part and parcel of a society dependent upon passive entertainment, labor-saving gadgets, and quick, technical "solutions" to human, existential problems. The couple that turns on the television and proceeds to watch three or four hours together is deriving about as much building material for their relationship as their bodies derived from the junk food they grabbed at the local market before hurrying home to watch that latest television show. The artificial stimulants and passive entertainment—from alcohol to drugs, from television to movies to quadrophonic stereos to rock concerts—with which our society is overflowing do not provide the fundamental ingredients of self-reliance, effort, and mutuality that love relationships have required from the dawn of the human adventure. In a society that makes everything easy, love becomes very hard.

Doing meaningful activities together, therefore, isn't so easy a proposition as our troubled couple might think. Much of what we have come to regard as "normal" activity is quite

31

abnormal or unnatural from permanent love's perspective. Just as a couple's very ideas of love and relationship may revolve around stimulation and passive self-gratification, so their notion of what one does as a couple is deeply infected with the easy-way-out psychology. Such a couple should be well-advised that their initial forays into sharing strengthening behavior will be fraught with the pain of easy gratification denied and with the ever-present temptation to go back to the familiar, the weakening, the easy-to-do.

A lot of couples whom I counsel follow a familiar scenario of activity in their marriage. In replying to my question, "When was the last time you did something enjoyable alone together?" they will travel back to the early years of their marriage when they played tennis or shared a hobby or fixed a meal. Gradually, imperceptibly, the internal and external temptations toward the easy way prevailed. Affluence brought not just color televisions in profusion but all manner of mechanical gadgetry and an increasing access to passive entertainment. Not fully understanding what their wedding vows or their original intentions and promises to each other really entailed in the arena of life and the unfolding of time, the couple slowly surrendered vital components of their activity together until eventually their relationship was reduced to a set of stereotyped and superficial interactions.

But let's ground these abstractions in the concrete reality of everyday life. A couple, call them Frances and Charles, has come to see me. They're fairly young—in their early thirties—and have been living together for the last three years. Having come of age in the sixties, Charles and Frances are "tuned in" to the lifestyles and expectations that we associate with that decade.

"I can't understand it, the feeling has gone out of our relationship. Charles doesn't turn me on like he used to. It's kind of dull living with him." Frances speaks her mind right off the bat. Her friend is more passive. I have to ask him to respond to this assertion. "Yeah, same with me. It's boring; there's nothing to our relationship anymore. I don't hate her, but there's nothing there anymore. Maybe we've just fallen out of love."

I've long since learned that apparent apathy and unresponsiveness, the frequent use of words like *boring* and *dull*, don't necessarily mean what they appear to. The couple probably would not have lasted three years, nor come to see me, if a strong core of care and commitment didn't underlie their listlessness. Their words and their manner indicate the way they are accustomed to reacting to stress and the way they express themselves, but the words cannot necessarily be taken at face value.

Questioning uncovers the fact that they were happy when they were first involved. Then they enjoyed their shared activities—horseback riding, swimming, taking the same adult education classes, and doing the same household tasks. The first year of their relationship saw them frequently engaged in these relatively strenuous and demanding pursuits. Indeed it laid the base for the strength that got them through the next two years without breaking off their attachment. I ask them, "What do you do now?" Frances's answer reads like a composite of a hundred similar answers I've heard from young lovers over the last seven or eight years.

"Well, Charles watches television a lot. We go to the movies fairly often. We turn on [to pot] quite frequently and listen to music. We have a great new stereo system. My mother hasn't been feeling good lately, so I've started

33

spending a lot of time with her. Charles sees his friends on the weekends, and we seem to go to a lot of parties with them. Lately we've started bickering with each other when we're alone. I don't know. . . things aren't what they were, that's all."

How they got from Point A, three years ago, to Point B, today, I don't know. (I never ask "why?" of clients; it leads to verbal quicksand faster than anything I know. I can only discover the why slowly. And the answer isn't important anyway at the therapeutic level, though it is sometimes curious.) Watching television, smoking pot, succumbing to the stereo is a lot easier than taking classes or going to the stables early on Saturday morning. The circumstances of life change—jobs have to be held down; a household supported. The internal dynamics of a relationship change, too—sex becomes familiar, if not routine; the first, ecstatic stage of getting to know someone is swiftly passed; hidden pockets of conflict open up, and so on. Any number of perfectly normal factors might have nudged Charles and Frances away from investing the money, time, and energy that their early activities together demanded. Perhaps the strength-building activities in question truly did become impossible to pursue after the couple was obliged to support themselves (though they might then have found replacements). In any case, they did not realize how important this kind of shared interaction was to their love; and nothing in their backgrounds or formation would have taught them otherwise.

Like all too many young couples, Charles and Frances imagined that the goal of life—certainly of one's love life—was pleasure, good feelings. While in a manner of speaking this may be true (who marries for pain?), the degree of effort and strength required to produce lasting, profound pleasure in

34

the form of an enduring relationship was unknown to them. Strength may indeed produce pleasure; but all pleasure does not necessarily produce strength. The first year of their marriage was a time of pleasure and strength for Charles and Frances. But as the basis of strength-building activity evaporated, *the pursuit of passive pleasure proved increasingly inadequate to sustain their relationship.*

Music, drugs, television, sex, and parties do indeed create a form of togetherness; and they certainly generate pleasure. The togetherness is illusory, however, and the pleasure is not, in itself, particularly strength-building. (Nor is it bad; it simply does not contribute to founding a deep, lasting relationship between people. In a context of strength, these passive pleasure-producing activities would be perfectly fine.) The togetherness that immersion in music or television produces is illusory because it requires no mutuality or united *effort from the participants.* They may as well be apart; and, indeed, in their separate, self-gratifying reaction to a particular stimulus they are quite apart. Even in sex—a topic I shall deal with presently—the activity, *by itself*, does not normally build anything between the participants (though it may give great pleasure).

So what? Specifically, how does Charles and Frances's relationship suffer from the fact that they're no longer swimming or horseback riding together? A shared strength-building activity carries with it the unconscious awareness that the pair is accomplishing something. Even a game requires a mutuality of effort and concentration, which unites the doers as they do. The game creates a context in which knowledge of one another is gained together with confidence in the relationship. Constantly shared effortful activity quietly instills the awareness in the couple that they can do

35

something in tandem. They are equal to various tasks. This makes for mutual confidence. It also creates the feeling that comes from the internal recognition that together they can make it.

What kind of communication? Did you ever paint a room with someone very dear to you? Or build a bookcase? Or organize a program of some kind? Were you silent during the interaction? Of course not. But you weren't concentrating on yourselves, individually or as a couple, were you? As you worked and assisted one another, you interacted *semiconsciously*. For some reason, *that kind* of interaction over a long period of time is worth its strength in rivets for underpinning a relationship. It affords a completeness and togetherness that self-conscious trying would only inhibit. But this semiconscious process of giving and taking, adjusting and assisting, working and playing, talking and laughing, creates knowledge and confidence. Given enough of this kind of interaction, you gradually come to have a very deep picture not only of who-I-am but also of who-I-am-with-you. More than that, you-and-I takes on a reality that previously you and I had separately. Our relationship assumes a shared reality because we, two, accomplish something together—whether we build a bookcase or wallpaper a room. From that accomplishment comes a generalized confidence that mere shared stimulation, appetite satiation, or passive pleasure cannot create—the confidence that we, as a couple, are equal to problems, tasks, stress, growth, accomplishment.

Do you remember the book *The Inner Game of Tennis*, by W. Timothy Gallwey, which appeared a few years ago? An observant fellow, Gallwey noticed that in tennis, as in all things, we accomplish the activity with two selves—what he calls Self 1, the conscious ego state, which worries and tries, and Self 2, the body and the unconscious acting quietly together. Much as we need Self 1 for learning and communicating, the fact remains that Self 2 performs much more naturally and easily if Self 1 isn't constantly overseeing, judging, pressing. Applying Gallwey's insights and vocabulary to the subject before us, I have discovered that if one can learn to let go of Self 1 by surrendering noncritically to the activity at hand (assuming that the activity is strength-producing), then he is in an excellent position for his Self 2 and his lover's Self 2 to do some serious (and often pleasurable) growing, building, and communicating together.

People who are insecure, competitive, worried, and struggling tend to live exclusively in Self 1. They use Self 1 to create, control, and delimit their relationships with others. In play, as in sex, as in work, as in *everything,* they tend to remain self-conscious, laborious, oppressive. The whole concept of letting go is fearful to someone who feels he has to hang on, to be in the saddle, to be always alert to getting his share. Yet although this is how many of us try to operate, it is not actually how life is lived in the long run. The fact is, life for all of us, sooner or later, takes place at the semiconscious level of Self 2. We cannot keep sentries posted forever in our minds. If only we realized earlier that it is in the letting go—in the trusting to life's (and to our own internal) process—that we will ever possess much of value, then we would spare ourselves (that is, our Self 1) an enormous amount of futile effort and heartache.

Certain kinds of activity permit the retirement of a couple's Selves 1. No matter how heated the emotion generated by squabbling and bickering, if you take a walk together after dinner, or play a set of noncompetitive tennis, or wash the dishes, or do a jigsaw puzzle together, the demands

37

of the activity will (given half a chance) tend to suck you both into the activity itself. Your Selves 2 will emerge, interact, and create patterns of interaction, which will (if allowed to continue) start to undercut the problems of Selves 1. The real weakness of most relationships is that as the frequency and quality of Self 2 interaction diminishes, the couple tries to compensate with increased Self 1 communication and solutions—that is, arguments, discussions, vows, programs, promises, counseling. Nine times out of ten, however, what is needed is something a lot simpler than that. Assuming that your conscious selves are fundamentally committed to the relationship, they (Selves 1) need not be consulted again for the weeks or months it takes to reintroduce Selves 2 to each other and permit Selves 2 some time apart.

I remember one gay couple who came to see me. The one man was nearly twelve years older than his friend, who was still in graduate school. Highly intelligent, spiritual, and emotional young men, the two were also somewhat insecure and inexperienced in relationships. Characteristically for such intellectual, verbal people, they had literally talked themselves into an overly "profound," overly "meaningful" commitment well before they had had the opportunity to let it happen naturally. In Gallwey's language, they were both strongly Self 1 personalities—which was ironical, because upon questioning them, I realized that the times they most enjoyed together were the unconscious moments of sharing in the writing of a series of newspaper articles. It required only a few sessions of counseling to set them on the road to reorienting the nature and quality of the time they spent together—no more heavy talks or arguments followed by impulsive declarations; instead, more shared work and recreation. Nothing changed overnight, but quite quickly

38

both men understood and appreciated the magic of losing themselves together in a shared activity in order to find their relationship.

* * *

People ask me regularly if I would draw up a chart of strength-building activities, or at least propose criteria that would define such activities. While I shall presently advance some ideas in this matter, I should say at the outset that ultimately it doesn't matter much what specifically you decide to do together as long as the activity meets the requirements we have talked about—that is, to develop couple-knowledge and mutual confidence at a semiconscious level. The activities you choose to pursue must suit the contours of your personal relationship at the time you decide to undertake them. In the case of Charles and Frances, the point was not that they had to resurrect horseback riding and swimming, or enroll in university extension courses together. The requirements and limitations of their conjugal lives no longer permitted that kind of expenditure of time or money! Thus it doesn't matter what you do as long as it permits the occasion for mutuality and effort. Much more important than *what* you do is *that* you do something and do it regularly. The Mormon Church has the institution of Family Home Evening. The church supports this regular Monday-night event with a formal program of readings, suggested activities, and so on. Less formal, but still encouraged by that church, is Sweetheart Evening, on Friday nights. What I am saying is that married couples need their regular time together too.

What is a relationship after all, anthropologically
speaking? What historic purpose has it served in the evolution
of mankind? Procreation, pleasure, and spiritual
considerations aside, relationships—and I mean this in the
larger sense of human bonding, whether male/female,
male/male, or female/female—have existed because isolated
individuals aren't equal to the task of survival. They need one
another's help and sustenance to make it through, to progress
and grow. Love has flourished, therefore, as the social cement
of relationships and patterns of interaction that society has
needed to survive and grow.

A delectable morsel for people who savor irony is this.
Society has largely succeeded in winning the battle of
economic survival and thus has freed itself for other goals, the
most important being the quest for relationships and love. But
now people are finding relationships and love harder to create
and hang on to. It's as if human history were trying to remind
us that we cannot expect to build our relationship with the
cement of emotions alone; we *still* need the building blocks of
shared activity toward a goal. Obviously, for most of us the
goal is no longer simply survival, but that doesn't mean that
the activities we share with our significant others cannot
entail (and would do well to include) what are—
anthropologically speaking—survival functions.

The other point is this. Permanent love is probably
impossible to arrive at *directly*. Anthropologically, as we have
seen, it is a *by-product* of something else, something both
larger and smaller than itself. The mistake our society is
currently making in its obsessive concentration on erotic
relationships is to overlook what relationships are
fundamentally built upon. This oversight only proves the
traditional Eastern (Oriental) insight that the more you seek

40

after something and yearn for it, the less likely you are to have it. Only in relinquishing your grip on some maniacal striving for a goal do you free yourself for the opportunity of achieving it. As true as this is for most things, it is essentially true of love and of love relationships. Love by its very nature resists compulsion and demand. Inextricably interwoven with freedom and choice, love and love relationships cannot long abide on terrain where freedom and choice are reduced by too much trying, despite the most fervent efforts, promises, and programs of conjugal exploration and "liberation."

Inevitably in the beginning, the activities you and your love undertake as a result of reading this book, or of seeing a counselor with a similar outlook, will prove somewhat artificial or difficult. If no interaction or enfeebling interaction has been your steady diet heretofore, strengthening activity may initially seem forced and useless. Strengthening activity is not the kind of miracle medicine that Esalen or Masters and Johnson or a thousand other therapists hand out. In fact it isn't medicine at all (unless we're talking about the preventive kind); rather it is activity based on common sense and hard work.

The first thing for deeply troubled couples to do is to clear small patches of ground in the crowded, confused arena of their overlapping lives—places where they can stand quietly alone together. The activity at this early stage, therefore, will be very simple: take a walk together after dinner, perhaps commenting simply on what you see around you (but not discussing your relationship!); play racquetball or go bowling twice or thrice a week; go for a swim; throw a frisbee; work in the garden. You see my point. Where the relationship is very fragile, stress-filled activity such as slaving over your tax form may prove too fraught with fight potential.

41

The first criterion, or checkpoint, then, of strength-building activity is that *it be shared* and that *it be done alone by the couple.* One of the reasons that the early years of a relationship are the happiest is that the lovers spend a lot of time alone together. Admittedly, much of this time may be given over to pleasurable, but not especially strength-building, activity. But usually there is a mix of both kinds of activity.

Unfortunately, in all too many cases, once the newness of the relationship—the jangled emotions and physical stimulation—wear off, the lovers take to the easy ways out that our society provides for people who don't like to make efforts; they commit themselves wholesale to distractions. It's not simply booze and pot that may come between lovers. Many couples, for example, have children right away and throw themselves completely into raising them, to the detriment of their own time together. Other couples will throw themselves into their work or the social scene, while others will wander off into the wasteland of nightly television or leisure technology. The first criterion in Step One, therefore, is to reunite the separated by reacquainting them with some of the earlier and better modes of their interaction.

One couple I counseled recently had spent *no time alone together* since the birth of their first child. The oldest was now four. "We thought doing things as a family was important," they said. "It is," I responded, "but not at the expense of your marriage and life alone together."

Other couples get together with friends on the weekend or join groups involved in various sporting or hobbylike activities. While all this is good, the fact remains, they must spend some time *alone* together. Every time a couple adds others to their activities, they tend to water down the strength-building process because *their own interactions with each other are what strengthen their lives together.* Social life is important, but it is not a substitute for time alone with each other.

The second criterion for strength-building interaction is that it be *continuous and increasing*—a growing part of the couple's lives. Even if the shared behavior starts out as nothing more than a walk after dinner, I insist that it be a *daily episode.* Ten or twenty minutes every day is worth more than three hours once a week. Short doses are good because they permit togetherness without risking a stressful confrontation before strength has been built into the fragile relationship. I insist, of course, that these daily fifteen-minute sessions are most certainly *not* occasions to discuss the troubles of the relationship or even to discuss anything having to do with the relationship. What we want is to maximize the retirement of Selves 1 and the emergence of Selves 2 on a steady, progressive basis.

I had a couple come to me who had already separated. They were committed to saving their relationship, to be sure, and they had wisely decided to separate for just that reason. I made no attempt to bring them back immediately into cohabitation. They literally could not be together for more than an hour without hair-raising battles ensuing. In the first counseling session with them, I learned that their most memorable moments of happy interaction had occurred years before when he played the guitar in accompaniment to her piano playing.

We agreed by the end of the session that the husband would come over once a day after the children were bedded down for the night, and the two of them would perform their music together for twenty minutes. Off they went. The next evening I got a call at home. (I always make myself available to my clients twenty-four hours a day, although my sour disposition is directly proportional to the lateness of the hour they call.) "John says I can't read music, that blockhead!" were the first words I heard as I answered the phone. Out tumbled a few hundred more ill-chosen epithets derogating her husband. I waited impatiently to get a word in.

"How long were you playing?" I asked finally.

"Well, he was here for over an hour," came the reply, "and we were having a great time until he told me I couldn't read music, that blockhead!"

"What was the plan we agreed upon?" I asked.

"Well, we were having such fun. . ."

"What was the plan?"

"Twenty minutes."

"Well, then, stick to the plan."

Even when things are going well, a couple within a fragile relationship cannot handle too much time together. But in a strong marriage, I believe a half hour a day is the *absolute minimum* a couple should be alone together. I find in my own marriage that when I see myself getting irritated at Hester, I immediately check on our time alone together and *always* find I have been slacking off. In a sense, my irritation is my warning system telling me I am ignoring my wife.

A third criterion of strength-building behavior is that both *parties should be aware of one another*, ideally should need each other, in the performance of the activity at hand. The musical duo just described exemplifies what I mean: the interaction was serious (though pleasurable), requiring mutual contribution to a whole that was larger than the sum of its parts. The main point is that the activity not only should bring you physically together, but should also create a

44

consciousness of each other as you work or play. Water skiing, tennis, hiking, monopoly, cribbage, ping-pong are good examples.

A couple I once counseled had begun making leather articles to sell, such as shoes, purses, belts. All went well until the husband went selling on the road. The wife became overwhelmed by the sheer volume of business, and soon the couple found themselves doing little together. They became more involved in the business and less aware of each other. Another couple I knew became so engrossed in perfecting their tennis game that they forgot they had to be partners in other areas, too.

Absence and presence among human beings are more than physical experiences. You are all the more present to me when I am trying to please you or help you or teach you, or whatever. An office worker may feel he knows the boss much better than he knows the mailboy because the boss is someone whose goodwill counts a good deal more in his life than the mailboy's. And consider this: our sense of getting to know another person depends greatly on how much we have done *for* that person. Why else is it that parents so often feel they know their children well, while children feel they and their parents are strangers? The parents have done much *for* the children, and that gives them a sense of knowledge about them. The children, having done little for the parents, may feel remote from them, even alienated. Sometimes, after years pass, these children, whose parents may now be ailing or dependent, feel that now, yes, they know their parents quite well, while the parents feel that the children they once knew so well have become strangers to them. So this principle can have mixed results between parent and child, but a married couple can almost always use it to good effect. The more each does *for* the other, investing time and effort, the better each will feel he or she knows the other.

On the other hand, being the recipient of someone's loving attention, when it is given as an equal, can provide a great sense of strength. When children sense the loving presence of their parents, they grow in their sense of self-worth and feel they have the strength to take risks in life. Lonely and discouraged people can derive this strength from the attention of a caring therapist, but they will fail to derive it from an uncaring therapist. When I am counseling, I sometimes become indifferent to a given client. I may try to hide my indifference, but invariably the client notices it. I once had a client say, "I really don't think you care anymore"; and though I protested, I realized that, yes, I *had* slacked off and I now had to work a little harder if I was to help this client. I saw the same principle at work in a mental hospital where I was a consultant. Some of the mental patients changed simply through perceiving the effort exerted for them by the staff. And yet I must repeat: the greatest change occurs not in the receiver but in the giver. I once asked a group of teachers who had been employing methods I had taught them with their students what had been the biggest resulting change. "The biggest change was in me," one said; "I have changed the most."

This leads to the fourth criterion, which is closely related: it is best if the activity *permits the use of human reason, of skill or creativity, and certainly of effort.* Remember that the underlying prizes we are seeking are couple-knowledge and couple-confidence. These qualities can occur only if the partners are setting themselves to a task that demands a certain amount of effort, reason, ability. How do I reveal myself to another or build self-confidence except as I mobilize and put to use the best that is within me? Likewise, there is no better way for a couple to come to know each other profoundly, to build a confident sense of "we-ness," except as they do something together that mobilizes their individual resources of mind, heart, spirit, and body.

Thus, as important as it is to start out a program such as this with "bite-size" chunks that are simple to assimilate (for example, evening walks together), I very quickly try to get the partners to undertake more challenging activities, activities that will build greater confidence and afford greater knowledge of themselves than just walking or playing would.

I know a young couple who recently married after living together for a couple of years. Mark and Julie started their relationship with far less in common than they have now built. The usual bundle of imponderables brought them together—physical attraction and compatibility; desire for security; the mutual stimulation of two vibrant personalities; and so on. He was a doctor, she a nurse, but they worked in totally different locations and settings. Gradually Mark's hobby, running, became a shared hobby. Mark and Julie began running together. Within a year, Mark became very interested in the physical and psychological benefits of jogging, and he started to employ running therapy in his work with heart patients, overweight cases, and depression cases among others. Julie seized on Mark's ideas, and the two of them worked out a program whereby she could use running therapy in her professional work with cardio-pulmonary rehabilitation patients. Her work was so successful that she was written up in the local press, as was Mark.

Mark and Julie's relationship became extraordinarily strong because of their mutual interest in jogging. What had been a fun hobby was now a stout plank, helping to build confidence and identity as a couple. This isn't to say that they, like every other couple, don't still have problems to work out and stress to confront. But they now come to those problems and encounter that stress with the additional assurance born of their track record (so to speak). They know they can build and interact; they have living proof that they can work as a team. Their sense of "we-ness" isn't simply dependent on vows and sex and security needs; it is anchored in the daily, ongoing process of building something precious to both of them.

All relationships, no matter how deep they may be, can be deepened still further by additional shared meaningful activity. You simply don't know a person really well until you have sweated, pondered, grunted, tried, failed, and succeeded with him. There is something about the process of building together that exposes you to another person in revealing ways that mere nakedness could never do. Steve and I thought we knew each other, felt we loved each other, before we began writing together two years ago. Indeed, at a certain level— which now seems rather superficial to both of us—we did. But the experience of writing two books together has given us a confidence in our "we-capability," which transfers over into all areas of our interaction. Previous sore points—Ed's stubbornness, Steve's inconsiderateness; Ed's predilection for superlatives, Steve's skeptical sarcasm—are more easily tolerated than before. The irritations and confrontations they occasionally led to are now quickly resolved. The underlying purposiveness and mutuality of the friendship—the rocklike respect and assurance that our shared activity instills in us—provides a kind of all-weather pliability in our interaction that nothing else could give.

From these examples you may think I am implying that

48

the only viable love relationships are those that are anchored in shared work. Without meaning in any sense to undervalue the utility of the latter, let me say, however, that everyone doesn't have to be Marie and Pierre Curie or Will and Ariel Durant to have a good marriage. No single kind of activity— be it work, play, child rearing, or conversation—is in itself *sufficient* to create permanent love.

Thus, in strong relationships, a myriad of shared activity invariably unites the lovers. Shared work is obviously a wonderful link, and I urge you to consider ways of coming closer to your lovers in your work and theirs (work defined both in the narrow professional sense and in the broader sense of any serious goal-oriented or problem-solving activity). But there are many other strength-building activities as well, such as amateur theater, fine arts interests, backpacking, gardening, political campaign work, church functions, volunteer work, dancing, exercise, sports, collecting (rocks, insects, stamps), patronship and philanthropy, photography, bird-watching, furniture refinishing, carpentry, reading and discussion seminars, or participation in civic affairs. There are dozens of others,[1] of course, and you will have to assemble a "package" that suits your relationship. I have purposely not mentioned activities like housekeeping or child rearing (which couples will automatically be obliged to undertake together), not because they cannot be relationship-enhancing, but because they are unavoidable duties and they do not ordinarily permit the couple to be alone as a couple in the activity.

Some people will view my suggestions in this chapter as so much busy work. These people may imagine that I'm trying to turn lovers into busy bees who follow schedules and check criteria, who garden here, study librettos together there,

49

devalue sex and fun, disdain television, and so on, *ad nauseam*. Well, since it won't help to deny such intentions, permit me on at least one or two counts to enter a plea of guilty. In my experience as both husband and professional counselor, I have seen the effects of the distorted view of love that society has foisted upon us and which it exploits daily. And, yes, I am guilty of wishing to expose that travesty. Romantic or sexual love, as we are led to conceive it, is a thing apart from life, promising a special set of unrealistic, unfulfillable expectations from a goddess- or god-like partner and an event that "happens" to us (we "fall" in love) as if our free will and reason—present elsewhere, in other relationships and activities—were suddenly suspended. Love is a thing we worship and cultivate as *the* source of personal stimulation, growth, discovery; it is our resort, our island in the stream, our separate peace from life's wars. Hogwash. That may indeed be what love is for all too many people, but that is precisely why permanent love, as we have been speaking of it in this book, is an increasingly disappearing anomaly.

Love does not need to be fantasized to be the remarkable, wonderful, life-gracing thing that it is. It does not need to be packaged and idolized; rather it needs very badly to be reintegrated into the common stream of life whence it sprung and in which it constantly draws its sustenance. Romantic love, especially, needs to rediscover its link with other human love—with friendship, for example. How many friendships do you know that have far outlasted romantic relationships? Very many, I would wager. This may partly be due to the innate volatility of the sexual tie, I admit, but we have made that volatility and transience a thousand times more potent by the ways we have detached romantic love from its sources.

What I am saying is this: in the truly basic love relationships of our lives, we cannot hope to make it on the superficialities of romantic love alone. If these relationships do not flow out of the major streams of our life's course, they will sooner or later fail to stay meaningful in our life's changing context. A romantic commitment cannot somehow expect to sit on the bank and watch the lovers' lives flow by. If the relationship isn't sailing on the river—risking, tacking, checking constantly for depth, watching for snags, studying the currents and winds—then it will eventually lose its relevance and be bypassed.

Perhaps now the reader will better understand my heavy-handed emphasis on activity, on behavior. This emphasis is the only antidote to society's vastly more powerful overemphasis on feelings, fantasy, and stimulation. If love is to be rescued, the rescue operation must entail a demystification, a homey, down-to-earth attention to mundane things; for *these are the sources of the feelings of love*—the feelings that say (*especially under stress*) *we can make it, we can work out a better way*. We may not be able to master our feelings all the time, but we can master our actions fairly successfully. Hence we can exercise control, decision, will, and choice in the matter of love. We can and we must.

* * *

A word about sex since no book that purports to speak about romantic love can avoid it. Since sex is very much an activity "you can do together," now seems the logical time to raise the topic. Lest in what follows I be mistook for a prude,

51

let me say now: *I like sex a lot.* So does Hester. I can easily share the sentiments of the noted poet Adrienne Rich:

> *I'd call it love if love*
> *didn't take so many years*
> *but lust too is a jewel.*

The problem with sex from our perspective is that society has made it into a breeding ground of illusions. Alone and unadorned, the sex drive is powerful enough—"one of the three or four prime movers of all that we do and are and dream, both individually and collectively," wrote Philip Wylie in his remarkable *Generation of Vipers*. But in the social trappings with which we have burdened it, the sex urge and the sex act confuse, almost hopelessly, the reality of permanent love in the public eye. Other appetites are powerful, yet we manage to satisfy them without swamping ourselves in illusions about them. Nobody who is hungry, for example, would sit down to a banquet and be tempted in his rapture to confuse his stomach's craving with the hunger of the soul or the mind. He would enjoy his eating and the conviviality of his fellow eaters, and that would be the end of it. Sex, however, is another matter. The emotional and psychological charge that it carries far outdistances its actual power to provide heat and light, that is, to create or sustain love.

Forgive me for being so provocative and blunt, but sex has almost nothing to do with love. It may indeed be one of the major drives that draws two people together so that love, perchance, may arise; and it is undoubtedly one of the most ecstatic by-products and reflections of permanent love. But it is not love and, by itself, has little to do with love. Ultimately, whether we like to admit it or not, sex is the

fulfillment of an appetite; it is self-gratifying and object-
oriented (that is, it objectifies the human being by focusing on
the body alone). Love, on the other hand, is ultimately
indifferent to body and appetite; it focuses on people as
subjects, not objects, and is self-giving. Love is a continuous
action and pattern of behavior involving the whole self (not
merely the emotions or the drives) and centered in the will
and the spirit.

Love is not hostile to sex; nor is sex, per se, hostile to
love. They simply move in different spheres and have, in
reality, rather less to do with one another than they appear to
have at first (or second) glance. Sex does not by itself build
strength in a relationship because it is not, in the end,
committed to building a relationship but to gratifying an
appetite. Appetites, as we know, are powerful things, and,
very often, to leave them unsatisfied or inadequately satisfied
is to ruin a chance for permanent love; but then so would the
absence of food or sleep or oxygen ruin the chance of
permanent love.

It is not hard to see how sex breeds illusions, particularly
among young (would-be) lovers. The physical intimacy that
sex requires can easily be mistaken for profounder, more-
difficult-to-achieve kinds of mutual knowledge. The technical
adeptness of good sex can easily foster a false sense of
confidence in the relationship; and, in very young partners,
the simple fact of performing genital sexuality can produce the
illusion of maturity. Moreover, the intense good feelings that
sex arouses pass too often in our society for "true love,"
especially among the young. Love, as we know by now, is too
long-term a phenomenon to be dependent upon the feelings
generated by sexual attraction. Sexual feelings are much more
closely tied to appetites and their fulfillment, or to mood and

disposition. Sexual feelings rise and fall; the less intense feelings of love abide (though they must periodically deal with sexual feelings and their problems). Again it must be remembered that the feelings of sex differ from the feelings of love. Feelings of love come from the recognition that someone cares and that we can make it under stress together; sexual feelings come from physical attraction to, or satisfaction with, another person.

The reason that sex has become almost an obstacle to love is that too commonly in our society sexual desire must mask itself as love in order to accomplish its goal of seduction. The underlying Puritan ethic, which still informs a fair share of American mores, forbids directness in sexual matters. Men and women, girls and boys, may pursue each other, but the motivation has to be dressed up as love-seeking and relationship-building. This isn't simply a ruse or a game; all of us *actually believe it* to a greater or lesser degree. We become sexually involved with someone and we honestly think we are, or want to be, or ought to be, *in love* with them. Having no idea of what love is anyway—no notion of the long-term character or the dimensions of will, mind, spirit, and behavior that determine love—we cannot help but define love in the media-prescribed, mesmerizing ways.

Once "in love," therefore, we promptly go about phonying ourselves up in ways we are told will attract our "beloved." We doctor our appearance, perfect a "line," and generally alter our behavior, style, dress, activity—sometimes gravely distorting our real identity—in an attempt to be "sexy." A relationship built on such an artificial base cannot help but reflect the phony behavior and underlying motives of seduction by which it was constituted. And this is what we call "love." Small wonder then that we become deeply

54

involved with a romantic partner without, for the longest time, having any authenticity in the relationship. The lack of authenticity is covered up by the exultant stimulation of our physical closeness, by the apparent intimacy of the "deep" conversations, by the seismic readings given off on the Richter Scale of our emotions. And so "love" progresses—too many of us walking to the altar, supported by family and social expectations, or at least entering into a formal conjugal relationship on such a basis. For all the world, we believe that we are on the road to permanent love, when, in reality, the habits of interaction we have created have less to do with permanence or love than with appetites, emotions, and social prescriptions. As long as sexuality remains at or near the focal point of the relationship, the surrounding jungle of emotions, drives, and conventions will prevent the relationship from settling down and becoming truly reflective and integrative. As long as sexuality remains at or near the focal point of the relationship, the likelihood that either partner will understand his own and his partner's true value, or construct patterns of interaction building upon and heightening that understanding, will remain minimal and accidental.

One proof of these contentions is the peculiar and intense sensation of let-down people frequently experience after the sex act. The anticlimax is the voice of our inner recesses of heart, mind, and soul reminding us that the physical stimulation, for all its flamelike intensity, cannot live up to the wildly unrealistic expectations we have laid upon it, nor is it worth the high price of self-distortion we may have paid for the seduction. The "down" wouldn't happen except that the "up" was too high, too much the creation of fantasy and anticipation. To clarify, let's return to our ravenous eater. If he encumbered the banquet with all manner of unrealistic hope for fulfilling needs far beyond his hunger, would he not suffer a massive depression when, in the wake of his satiation, nothing was filled but his stomach?

There is one important disclaimer to be made—a kind of exception that proves our rule about sex. If the partners work together to solve a sexual problem, that effort itself can build strength in their relationship. Sexual blockages— frigidity and impotence being the most common—can quickly imperil the closest relationship (in the same way that a short circuit can imperil the recorded performance of an opera). Sex, like oxygen or water, is fundamental to the body, even though it is not important to the relationship. If a sexual problem exists, the couple may be well-advised to work on it together.

But not directly on the specific problem. Once again we are back to the paradoxical situation where the best way to hold on is to let go, or, more aptly, the best way to regain a hold is not to try for it. If the frigidity, impotence, or lack of sexual enjoyment is really serious, no amount of unremitting gentleness or technical innovation is going to help very much anyway. Few actions reflect our own inner harmony or disharmony or our authentic or inauthentic ways of relating to our lover more closely or quickly than sexuality. The increase of sexual dysfunction, therefore, has a lot to do with the increasingly artificial and overcharged role that sex occupies in our psyches and our relationships. In short, sexual problems are the symptoms, not the cause.

The couple's best approach to sexual problems, thus, is to "end-run" them, so to speak, by going back to Step One (of permanent love) and reconsidering what they are doing together as a couple. After all, why has their sexual life gone awry in the first place? Is it connected (as it usually is) with

56

the weakness of their interaction? If the couple's relationship has been oriented only (or mainly) toward sexual intercourse, then very probably their excessive concentration on sex or their unrealistic expectations of sex has led to some psycho-sexual malfunction. Or if the weakness of their interaction is more diffuse than simple overemphasis on sex—say, for example, that the couple is drifting apart because all they do is watch television together or sit around or go to parties, movies, or social events—the first sign of that weakness will often be seen in their sex life.

To a counselor, few successes are more enjoyable than watching a couple solve a frustrating sexual problem by agreeing temporarily to shelve the problem itself and concentrate on their basic relationship. As they rediscover the strength of their partnership, sex returns to its proper place, and the couple then discovers what all true lovers know—the reward for putting sex in its place is that it becomes far more wonderful than it was when it tried (and failed) to occupy center stage.

NOTES:

[1] Edward E. Ford and Robert L. Zorn, *Why Be Lonely?* (Niles, Ill.: Argus Communications, 1975), pp. 67-70.

STEP TWO:

What You Can Do On Your Own

Just as the best way to solve sexual problems or deal with the tumult of conflicting feelings is often to lay them aside and deal with more fundamental issues, so the best way to help a troubled relationship is often to put the relationship itself aside and concentrate individually on the life and identity of each partner. A whole is the sum of its parts, but sometimes for the sake of mathematical (or therapeutic) operations, we have to break a whole down into its constituent parts and concentrate on them. The strength of a good union is the product, the mutual creation, of both lovers; but if the lovers, as individuals, do not bring strength to the union in the first place, they are not in a position to create relational strength, or couple strength.

In the steps to permanent love, therefore, we cannot overlook the crucial importance of the individuals *as individuals* in a relationship: the parts of the whole. In our discussion of the first step, we examined the main source of the strength of the whole—what a couple does alone together. Now it is time to examine the components of individual strength to see how they relate to the building of the whole. Before we are lovers, before we are colleagues, before we are parents or friends or brothers or sisters, we are individuals alone. We must never lose sight of this aloneness. If strength does not flow from it, then strength can never grow in the relationships we maintain and in the varieties of love we will be called upon to build. We can see this principle at work in the marriage of Marge and Jim.

Marge was twenty-one when I first met her. Shy, dependent, insecure, she came to see me because "my marriage is going to pieces, and I want to know what I can do to save it." Nearly three years before, at eighteen, Marge had married Jim, a man rather older than she (he was then twenty-five), and had given herself over to taking care of him. In doing so, she became highly dependent on her husband. This worked well enough at first while Marge learned how to anticipate Jim's every wish and need. But her husband gradually lost interest in the relationship and began spending increasing amounts of time away from home—at work, with his friends, playing sports. Marge responded by trying even harder to fulfill what she second-guessed to be her husband's expectations. It did not work, however. In fact, Jim began to reduce even the amount of affection and personal attention he gave her. Marge's self-esteem, never her strong suit in the best of times, fell off proportionally and finally hit rock bottom.

Jim was not interested in coming to see me (he did not

regard the marriage as particularly problematic), so I was obliged to work with Marge on her own. But even if Jim had been eager to work at reconstructing his marriage, I would have chosen to counsel his wife independently. This marriage was a classic example of an instance (and there are many) where Step One cannot be taken (or is not sufficient) because one or both of the partners of a love relationship is unwilling to work at creating strength in that relationship. Marge had been to several counselors before me, and they had been willing to operate on the same assumption that motivated Marge: What can a wife do to please her husband? (In fairness to my colleagues, I should say that it is sometimes nearly impossible to avoid dealing with, if not accepting, the client's definitions, assumptions, and frames of reference.) Marge, though depressed and timid, was initially remarkably tenacious about insisting that her approach was the only possible one. In listening to Marge's answers to my detailed questions about her marriage, however, I realized that before we could possibly tackle the problem of her relationship with Jim, we would have to attend to the more pressing issue of creating strength in Marge. That process could not be hinged on a program of serving Jim. Marge had to work at something from which she could experience immediate results and see improvement—something over which she had total control.

It was not an easy deal to get Marge to talk about her own life apart from the marriage to Jim. She had little to say about the matter, having given no thought to it. Indeed, as I strongly suspected, Marge had very little life or identity apart from her primary love relationship. In this she typified many thousands of young people whose selfhood is so inadequately developed as to require another person to prop it up and provide fulfillment. Marge, like many of us, used romantic

61

love as a drunk uses a street lamp—not for light, but for support.

This dependency was encouraged by Marabel Morgan in her books, *The Total Woman* and *Total Joy*: "A Total Woman caters to her man's special quirks; whether it be in salads, sex, or sports," followed with the prescription, "Tonight, after the children are in bed, place a lighted candle on the floor and seduce [your husband] under the dining room table."[1] The books have sold between them well over three million copies, so one is justified in gathering that they have struck a resonant chord among many more Americans than read *Ms.* magazine or the *New York Review of Books*.

Morgan appears to offer a haven for those women and men in this country who find the delivery of some feminists frightening and repugnant. The average housewife like Marge, whose horror of women's lib is the measure of her inner curiosity about it, now believes that she can find salvation from her failing marriage in the old-time religion (fashionably repackaged).

One does not begrudge Morgan her literary success or her audience. It is simply a tragic and characteristic irony of her brand of reaction that Morgan's "theory" and practice effectively betray the causes of conjugal and Christian love that she hopes to serve. If only Marabel Morgan had been thoroughly and radically "old-time"; if only her reaction to the errors of the *Ms.* set had led her back to human history and biblical faith. Then she might indeed have found a resourceful, original reply to her adversaries, and she might have made a helpful contribution to her suffering sisters like Marge. *The Total Woman* offers nothing but the weary old bromide of orienting conjugal relationships around sex and its "aura," psychological dependence, and constricting socioreligious convention (which, as we shall see in the epilogue, is not the same thing as authentic biblical faith). Would that the great challenges of loving could be reduced to the listing of quirks to be catered to! Or that the diminishing duration and fulfillment of relationships like Marge and Jim's could be stemmed with imported negligees intended to return "sizzle to your marriage!" At least if there were some chance that wishing could make it so, that Morgan and her millions of readers could materially redefine what love is (and what long-term love relationships entail), then one would perhaps deplore her action but stand in awe of her power. As it is, however, love "abideth," as St. Paul tells us; it remains stubbornly itself. The lamentable impact of Marabel Morgans on the Marges of this world is that the latter are kept longer in the dark and further from the goal.

In talking with Marge, I discovered that she was disturbed by her financial dependency. Before she met Jim, she had held a fairly responsible position in a local department store, and the job had provided her with pleasure and a strong sense of self-worth. (Indeed, I wished she had had three or four years of working at that job before she met Jim. The relationship and the marriage might have progressed differently.) After marrying Jim, she agreed, at Jim's insistence, to quit her job and devote "all my time to my husband." She admitted, however, that even during the most pleasurable period of her marriage to Jim, she regretted not working and resented her total financial dependence upon her husband. This financial dependence mirrored her psychological dependence; but she was not yet willing to confront this, believing, as she did, that it was normal for the wife to be subservient.

Therefore, in launching our effort to build strength in

the Marge half of the Marge-Jim relationship, we were able to use Marge's willingness to go to work. Without yet fully understanding how it would help her marriage, Marge agreed that working would be better than staying at home. (Or, as she put it, "It can't make things worse.") Once decided, Marge threw herself into the new project with zeal. She got her old job back at the department store, and within a month or so she was informing me that she intended to take evening courses in marketing in order to improve her prospects of promotion.

Weekends remained a problem: "They're so dull because Jim spends all his time with his friends." I suggested a number of things Marge might do with her weekend time. At first she was still interested in devising ploys to get Jim to stay home or take her along with him and his friends. But as that proved fruitless, she began to consider other alternatives. Ultimately she chose to serve as a volunteer driver for unsighted people . The overflowing gratitude and approval of her handicapped charges provided Marge with needed esteem and human warmth outside of the marriage.

Five months passed before Marge spoke to me again about her relationship with Jim, and then the most pressing reason for bringing it up was that Jim himself had unexpectedly come to see me. "I couldn't help noticing that my wife was coming to see you," he began, "and I couldn't help noticing that she's changed quite a lot and gotten pretty active. I just wanted you to know that I'm also interested in helping to improve our relationship."

Jim's announcement made possible the beginning of Step One—a step that presupposes some mutuality of commitment and some individual strength on the part of the partners. Marge by now had become a different woman. (I confess that few clients produce so dramatic a change in their behavior and self-image as she did.) The single most notable difference to me was that for many months now, Marge had not felt the need to mention Jim more than in passing. It was not that she did not continue to feel strongly about him or to include him in her life. In fact, their conjugal sex, social, and domestic lives unfolded uneventfully during this period. Rather, she had turned her considerable concentration and energy onto laying the foundations of her own worth. In the best way possible, this was her contribution to the marriage.

Actually, what I had been doing with Marge was the necessary prelude to counseling a married couple. You cannot concentrate on collective strength until the individual constituents of the collective are in a position to provide the wherewithal. In the case of Marge and Jim, the absence of strength in the wife was radical. In such instances where one partner is obliged to recreate his or her whole self-image, there is no telling what impact this change will have upon the relationship when the moment arrives to deal with that question. As a matter of fact, it took Marge a lot of careful consideration to decide whether she wanted to proceed to build permanent love with the man whom she had married, but whom, (as she herself admitted), she hadn't "really loved" until now.

* * *

The principal theme of this chapter, illustrated in the story of Marge and Jim, is that *what you are on your own will contribute decisively to what you are together*. Permanent love requires that you be strong, and in a very real sense you cannot be strong *through* or *for* but only *with* another person. It would have done no good for Marge to embark on a campaign of self-improvement for the sake of holding on to Jim. The motivation there would have sprung from and lead to further weakness, further dependency.

This point is crucial and deserves further elaboration. Too many love partners remain secretly convinced at some profound level of mind or heart that the effort of building personal strength carries with it the promise of happiness in the relationship. To harbor this wish is to doom the program of personal strength building before it has begun. You cannot strike out for freedom by fettering yourself to a pillar. You cannot grow (or live) for another, but only for yourself. In the case of Marge, she could not love Jim (or anyone else) by holding on to him. She had to let go, had to refocus on the quite different (yet quite related!) question of *Marge* before she could even consider Marge *and* Jim. If she had not truly relinquished her original grip (and it was vice-like, let me assure you), if she had guarded the flame of dependency in her heart, then she would have stood to lose all that she had gained through her work, her school, and her charity in the event that Jim had stayed cold and indifferent or had wandered away from her entirely. She would have blamed herself because the expected goal for which she was striving had not materialized. She would have continued to invest her currency in Jim's actions, reactions, and wishes, instead of in herself.

What Marge had to learn, among other things, was the hard lesson of solitude. I remember her saying to me not long after we had begun our work together, "Ed, for the first time in my life I'm learning what it is to be alone and not be anxious

66

or lonely." I knew then that there was real potential strength in this woman. The capacity to *accept* the existential fact of human aloneness in the world, or even to endure it with grace, let alone learning to love solitude, is an increasingly rare commodity among people. Most of us regard our aloneness as a thing to suppress or to escape. The prime motivation for human society, from this perspective, is to try to build walls to keep out loneliness. What is kept away, however, is the strength of solitude, not the pain of loneliness, which insinuates itself into even the happiest of social situations. He or she who does not learn to deal with being alone is doomed to weakness *and* loneliness, just as those who accept solitude and make creative use of it stand to discover some of the richest spiritual and intellectual treasures accessible to human beings.

Life would be easier if we could completely leap the barriers of flesh and mind that separate us from one another. It would be more bearable if a human being, out of love, could climb inside my heart, mind, body, and soul to shoulder the burden of conscience, the dilemma of indecision, the pain of physical injury, the turmoil of conflicting emotions. Life would be immeasurably easier if death and judgment were trials I could face with another man or woman, or if my anxiety and guilt could be parceled out among loyal friends. But as things are, the fundamental denominator of our reality remains, initially and finally, that finite individual called a human being. The only way to appreciate the triumphs (and understand the limitations) of culture and society—of the human *collectivity*—is to first accept this prior reality of individuality. More to the point, one can contribute significantly and satisfyingly to the collectivity only from the strength that comes with full acceptance of one's individuality, one's independence, one's aloneness.

Times of solitude are the occasions when one confronts one's aloneness. Solitude can be frightening for many of us. Marge, for example, hated it at first. Her relationship with Jim hinged on the illusory hope that she could escape accepting herself by becoming an adjunct of another person. For many years, I too hated solitude. It made me vaguely nervous, bored, anxious. I went out of my way to avoid being alone. It was hard to accept being alone, even in my religious and spiritual life. It took me a long time to learn to accept and value solitude, and then I did it, not by confronting solitude directly (which would probably have proved too difficult), but by encountering it as a by-product of an activity I greatly enjoyed—jogging. Gradually my daily runs grew in distance from one to seven miles, and my time alone from nine or ten minutes to an hour. A solid hour alone is a long time for most people. And by *alone*, I don't mean reading or watching television or writing a letter. I mean the real thing: just you and your thoughts.

It's difficult to describe what happens in extended periods of solitude or to delineate precisely the process by which strength is created. We are more narrowly concerned here with solitude's contribution to permanent love. And the nub of our argument is that solitude creates self-acceptance. But I surely don't mean that easily confected self-congratulation of the "growth centers." On the contrary, the initial experience of solitude (which may last for months and months) is that of a painful void which slowly undermines the brittle self-confidence we throw together to keep us going. Fantasies and self-delusions, beliefs and prejudices, defenses and roles—all tend to have a hard time crossing the desert of extended aloneness. One by one they start to fall away and expire in the strong sun of critical self-observation. The pain of their demise is still pain, even if it is growing pain. Nevertheless, self-acceptance will prove to be one of the many eventual rewards of frequent, chosen solitude, even if self-acceptance lies down a rocky road called self-confrontation.

Getting back to the perspective of permanent love, if time away is the necessary counterpart to the time you spend with your lover, then solitude is the great centerpiece of your time away. Out of all the things you can do by yourself to build strength and contribute to the relationship—getting a job, going to school, working for charity—creative solitude on a daily or semi-daily basis (in brief, endurable chunks) will be the most important. More than anything else, it will oblige you to see your love relationship for what it really is: two individual, separate entities (of strength) working at partially overcoming their separateness, yet not avoiding the fact of that separateness. You cannot depend lamely on another person and still come to value solitude and make creative use of it. Creative solitude is the mortal enemy of all urges, drives, and neurotic needs that undermine your independence, freedom, and strength.

A few practical hints for creative solitude. First, consecrate a place in your home or outside where you can be completely alone for a given time (not more than fifteen to twenty minutes a day initially, increasing to an hour or so over a period of four to six months). If setting aside a special time and place is too artificial or difficult, as it was for me, then choose an activity like running or knitting or gardening that you can do entirely unconsciously and in solitude. Meditation, yoga, or prayer are tougher forms of solitude, but very good.

Solitude can be compared to a high mountain: you

must ascend slowly or you will become discouraged and uncomfortable in the thin air. At first you might play music or, if necessary, read something spiritually or psychologically edifying. Soon, however, you will want to close the book, turn off the music, and be more completely alone. Let your thoughts flicker and meander as they will; let the waves of boredom crash over you without budging you. Boredom is your weakness's first line of defense against growth. Wait it out. Don't clock watch. In fact, remove timepieces from your place of solitude; your inner sense of what is needed will tell you when to stop. In general, try to remain in solitude for as long as it takes to attain a feeling of detachment from the stresses and stimuli of daily life.

Many people may be uncomfortable with this kind of total, empty solitude. But it is important that they give it an honest try. For those who still feel this way, there is an active solitude that is possible—working or playing alone at some activity. A fisherman, for example, may stand alone for hours on the banks of a rushing stream. If a trout strikes, he may bring home a meal. But if no trout strikes, he is still likely to bring home a spirit renewed in creative solitude.

In your solitude you will come to see how important independence, self-acceptance, and critical observation are to your own strength as an individual. Further, you will begin to see your lover apart from your own appetites, feelings, and reactions. And as this happens, your love will begin to become unconditional, that is to say, independent of the thousand and one things in daily life that make your feelings (not to be confused with your love) wax and wane. Unconditional love is the truest, best form of love because it comes from a centered self that is not vulnerable to the quakes and tremors of life—not even, in a certain sense, to your

70

lover's emotions and reactions. You will have a profound realization that you and you *alone* determine your loving despite the fact that you cannot control the world and the people around you.

We will hold off on further flights for the moment. There are a number of practical points left to be made in this chapter. For now, to quote St. Thomas More in *A Man for All Seasons*, "I trust I have made myself obscure." The epilogue will pick up where many of the untied threads of this "obscurity" have left off in the hope that by then, the several themes of our book will be woven together into one clearly visible tapestry.

* * *

So far we have been somewhat *self*-centered in this chapter, as if one's only obligation in this time and activity alone were to improve oneself while displaying kingly indifference to one's partner and relationship. But though it remains quite true that the foundation planks of individual strength consist of independence, self-reliance, freedom, and solitude, this is not to say that upon those planks we may not build patterns of behavior that focus on directly serving one's lover and the relationship (in that order of priority).

The lessons of the first part of this chapter were aptly illustrated by our friend Marge. By the time Jim came to see me, she was well advanced on the road to individual strength. Having started in a place where she had given away control over herself to another (Jim), she was now fast attaining the capacity to control her own will, mind, and feelings. She had, in sum, reached the point of being able to love Jim meaningfully. It was now up to her to decide how much she loved and whether she would continue to love. Falling in or out of love had nothing more to do with Marge. Love had become an expression of her will, or her self united, and the only decisions remaining for her were to determine whether she would tolerate Jim's behavior and attempt to pursue the creation of permanent love with him.

We have not forgotten about self-giving. It is still a vital part of love; *but it can be workable only when you have a strong self to do the giving.* In order for your giving to be truly altruistic, unconditional, and effective, it has to be without self-interest. It cannot be desperate, nor can it have strings attached—secret hopes to be realized or hidden agendas to be met. Attaching strings would mean that you were trying to control your lover's reactions to suit your own wishes. If Marge had used her newfound strength for this purpose, she would only have been reversing roles with her husband instead of building permanent love. Trying to change another for your own sake is hardly unconditional attachment. Your giving, therefore, must be genuine—for your lover's sake as well as for yours. In sum, giving must come from strength, not from weakness.

For many years I afflicted myself and my loved ones with a violent, ugly temper. I lost it unpredictably and easily, far out of proportion to the irritations and stresses that triggered it. I would hear myself yelling uncontrollably at my daughter Terry for lingering on the telephone, or I would stew in silence at my wife, Hester, for several days because she did not leave a party at precisely the (early) hour I wanted to leave. We had a good marriage; and both of us were committed to the relationship. Looking back now, I even realize that we

72

were practicing Step One of permanent love—that is, we participated in a fair amount of strength-building activities together. Still the matter of the temper remained, to everyone's chagrin.

Reading Bill Glasser's *Identity Society*[2] placed the problem in perspective for me. It didn't happen all at once, but one day, after reading over the questions "What am I doing?" and "Is it helping?," the pennies fell into the meter. A voice in my brain independently (it seemed) placed a strong emphasis on the pronoun *I*—what am *I* doing? I already had an intellectual understanding of the notion of individual responsibility for one's actions, but I had never felt its bite until then.

I began to ask myself, "What can I do on my own to improve my relationships with my wife and children? Putting aside the issue of *their* behavior and reactions, what can *I* do independently?" The question was all the easier to pose and to answer because, as I mentioned , we were already fairly well advanced in Step One (though I didn't call it that then). We shared a number of wonderful activities; the patterns of social interaction in my relations with my wife and children were active, not passive. But I continued to feel this strong desire to act independently—to make an individual effort and assert some self-determination as well.

So what did I do? I set myself the task of listing each day two things Hester said or did that were pleasing. It may seem simple-minded as a technique, but it counteracted quite well my tendency to concentrate on her irritating behavior. I resolved to smile on entering a room and finding her (or one of my children) there. Smiling was never one of my strengths (still isn't), and while the effort itself was easy, remembering to make it was hard. I increased my willingness to do

73

household chores. I left my wife little notes around the house—under her pillow, in her shoe, in a dresser drawer or a purse—expressing my affection or thanking her for a specific action or simply drawing a happy face. I kissed my wife every time I left or reentered the house. These were little, simple activities, you may say, but they required a good bit of effort and concentration from me.

Hester taught me early on the big lesson that everyone undertaking Step Two of permanent love must learn: Don't look for, expect, or depend upon, your lover's responsiveness to what you decide to do alone. Undemonstrativeness and understatement are Hester's style, and she didn't change it for me in gratitude for my behavioral innovations. In fact she said and did very little in response. I sulked a bit but persevered, reminding myself that I was choosing to do this independently of other people's reactions or lack thereof. Besides, what was I trying to do—change her or change myself? It was a personal exercise in will, and for a long while I proceeded on sheer will alone.

One day—just about the time when I had resigned myself to permanently unrewarded effort—I got a reward. Not from Hester, but from me. I felt my anger rapidly dissipate in an instance where normally it would have waxed hot. I was so pleasantly astonished that I pondered the phenomenon awhile. I realized that a lot of my previous anger was due to a feeling of helplessness. When things weren't going exactly my way (for example, if Hester wanted to stay at a party when I wanted to leave) that feeling was exacerbated, and I lost my temper in a futile effort to reassert my control over the situation.

Since I had begun implementing the decision to act on my own, however, the feeling of helplessness was evaporating.

I was obviously proving to myself that I wasn't helpless after all. Though I had no control over another person, I could (if I tried) exercise considerable control over myself (in this instance over my feelings) by changing my behavior. I realized that my anger was a sign, warning me that I wasn't showing my autonomy, my self-determination—that I was handing myself over to feelings and to other people's reactions and behavior. When that happened, my relationships with my loved ones were not well served.

In my pleasure at these little "victories," I added further to my list of activities to be performed "on my own." Sometimes, I added too many and had to regress a step or two. And sometimes, out of nowhere, my temper flared up like Old Faithful—though never for as long as before. The road to self-change[3] is long and winding, and although the general direction is upward, you sometimes have to descend. Mostly, however, you must keep walking, sustained by the internal recognition of your own success at figuring out a better way of accomplishing that change. Self-transformation is not usually as dramatic as that of St. Paul or Malcolm X or Martin Luther. But you'll notice that behavior patterns gradually realign and that feelings reluctantly, fitfully, but duly follow suit.

I want to emphasize, too, that profound self-change is not merely a question of a conscious roster of resolutions, as we are talking about in this part of the chapter. At the risk of sounding repetitious, I must reiterate that Step Two is possible only in conjunction with Step One. (Occasionally, Step Two is what gets Step One going.) If my life with Hester and my children had not been vigorously codeveloping in other ways than my little innovations, and if, for that matter, my efforts at improving my relationship with my wife and children were not matched by efforts to gradually reform my professional life (for example, I went back to graduate school full-time at the age of forty-four), then I strongly suspect the changes I now so highly value would not have taken place as swiftly—eight years being very "swift" as human change goes.

Now perhaps you can see a bit better how Step Two and Step One complement each other. What can you do if your lover seems not to want to do anything with you at a given moment? Must you be paralyzed when that happens? By no means. If you have developed some of the general, personal strengths we discussed in the introduction above, then you will be able to do something on your own to please your partner. So often we *feel* helpless. Anger, irritation, depression—most excessive displays of negative feelings in a relationship—are signs of that helpless feeling. But true helplessness, unless you are an inmate of a prison camp or a mental institution, is almost never justified. *You can always do something on your own* to improve the situation; the rampaging feelings, indeed, should indicate to you that you aren't doing enough. Put another way (which I learned from my friend Gary Applegate, a clinical psychologist), never give another person control over how *you* feel or what *you* do. By assigning the reason for my temper to my family's actions, I was giving them control over my feelings (anger) and behavior (rash statements, foolish gestures, and so on).

If you launch your efforts at self-change by expecting to retrieve, or hold, someone's love or responsiveness, your motivation for change will subside because you are placing yourself squarely under that other person's control. Shortly you will have to accept that you are truly acting *on your own* and for your own sake. Only thus will you have much hope of really contributing to your ability to make relationships with people work.

Having decided to act, then, you must select activities using your own judgment. Don't sit down with your partner and draw up a list that will meet his or her wishes. Be your own counsel. After all, it's not your partner whom you are trying to please; it's you whom you are trying to change and over whom you are trying to exercise control. (Only in doing this for yourself can you hope to please another in any lasting, strengthening way.) Nonetheless, the standards by which you must decide upon (and judge) your new behavior should not be indifferent or irrelevant to your partner's interests or to the cause of the relationship. On the contrary, you will undoubtedly (if you observe the situation clearly and critically) undertake activities that will more than introduce you to self-giving. I can't tell you specifically what things to do; I have presented an example from my own life in some detail. You must ask yourself, "What can I do to improve the situation?" and the question—if honestly posed—will beget honest, generous answers, which in turn will present self-evident patterns of behavior for you to incorporate into your life.

Ultimately, your activities are less important than their by-products. Accepting the need to act; exercising the will to act; choosing to think conscientiously about another person; exercising the creative faculties of reason to generate a plan; depending upon yourself for motivation and perseverance— these are the by-products that produce strength in self and hence in the self's love relationships.

They will also teach you a final lesson, which we'll be expanding upon at length later in of this book: You need the other person. That's right, I said *need*. But by now you can see I mean it very differently from what Marge meant when she spoke of her need for Jim. For if you succeed in creating independence, self-mastery, and unconditional love in yourself, you will ultimately realize that you owe these achievements to the other person; you needed that person— not so much for what he or she gave to you, but for the opportunity that your relationship provided for your own growth and self-transcendence. I once had an attorney call me, who was handling the divorce of a couple I had worked with. "I just called to let you know how much they said you helped them," he said. "They both claimed you taught them how to gain strength on their own, and, strangely enough, what loving is all about." Then he added, "That's the first time I have ever heard that." Permanent love permits, even demands, you to grow. I need Hester not for what she can do for me but for what she makes it possible for me to do with and for her. As Elizabeth Barrett Browning put it, "I love you not for what you are but for what I am when I am with you." A love partner is first and last an opportunity. The more I work at loving Hester, the fonder I become of her, the more I grow as a human being. By the same token, for her to grow in love, she has to work at loving me. That is the real paradox of love. When you marry, you do not acquire someone to provide you love as a sunlamp might provide you warmth. Marriage gives you nothing more than a fighting chance to make a lover of yourself. You can't stay in love by basking in your lover's affection as you might bask in the warmth of that sunlamp. Permanent love calls for more than that. Thus, you badly need the other person in order to be the best person you can be. *The only way you'll become your best person is by working hard at your love for the other.* Your love for others will come more from *your* efforts to love them than from the love they give you, as important as that is. Given love is vital when we are children; the examples of self-sacrifice shown by parents are what light the way for us to do the same. As St. Paul told us, however, "When I was a child, I spoke as a child, I understood as a child, I thought as a child; but when I became a man, I put away childish things." Childhood is the last, the only, occasion when we grow from passively receiving human love; thereafter the obligation shifts to our shoulders and stays there.

One final note. Many couples with whom I have worked have chosen not to stay together. The activity in Step Two teaches you to become more tolerant of others. But it may also help you to decide whether you wish your relationship to continue. Step Two builds strength, and as you realize that you now have more control over your own life and that you aren't totally dependent on others, you may decide to split up after all. But your decision to separate, in this case, will be the result of strength rather than weakness. Many couples decide not to live together and yet remain good friends. The activity in Step Two makes this possible.

NOTES:

[1]"The New Housewife Blues," *Time*, 14 March 1977.

[2]William Glasser, M.D., *The Identity Society*, rev. ed. (New York: Harper & Row, 1975), chap. 4.

[3]See *Why Be Lonely?*, chap. 3.

STEP THREE:

Conversation

We live in an age that glorifies communication. The art of conversation has become literally the science of communications. "Facilitating" communication has become the answer to nearly every personal problem and social conflict. If two sides clash over a principle or an interest, we assume that they simply aren't "getting through" to one another, they aren't "dialoguing" properly. The most common catchall cliché thrown up to me by troubled couples runs, "We can't communicate with each other." And conversely, the prevalent bromide used to demonstrate that two people are successfully relating is, "We have great communications—we talk about our feelings all the time."

If by *communications*, we mean nothing more or less than the systems of transmission of meanings among people, then I grant you that our society has indeed facilitated greatly such transmissions with our technology and social science. In fact, we have so facilitated and proliferated our systems of transmission that the media are now our cultural medium (or totem).

The problem, however, is that the transmission of meanings—the *form* of communications—so rivets our gaze and compels our collective imagination that we care very little for (and have very little originality to contribute to) the meanings transmitted—that is, the *content*, or *substance*, of communication. The technology of transmission overshadows, trivializes, buries the inscrutable, uncontrollable urges, meanings, and interactions that it was intended to "facilitate."

Love, in our age, depends heavily on communication for its style and its "strength." Current clinical and social psychology, not to mention the aging "growth centers," do a thriving business instructing people how to communicate more "honestly" and "effectively." In the absence of anything thoughtful or original to transmit to each other—that is, anything arising naturally out of the long-term sharing of strength-building activity—we have learned to communicate *about* love, *about* our "true" feelings, and *about* our relationship. We have also learned that sex is a "sacred" and "deep" form, perhaps the deepest form, of communication.

In sum, the way we communicate in our love relationships today faithfully reflects the culture in the special importance it attributes to frequent, "honest," "deep" verbal exchanges that have less and less to do with the natural transmission of meanings arising from shared activity and more and more to do with relieving or stimulating feelings, satisfying appetites, and creating appearances. As a culture, we are standing over a gigantic, growing gap between actions and words. One commiserates with Eliza Doolittle's lament, "Words! Words! Words! I'm so sick of words. . . if you're in love, show me!"

There's no reason to complicate a simple situation. It boils down to this: actions give rise to feelings; and feelings are a lot easier to talk about—to identify, reveal, and "express"—than action is to change. If our goal is to create good feelings, or—more likely these days—to escape bad feelings, then we may choose either the hard way out, which is lasting, or the easy way, which is temporary and spurious. The hard way is to alter the actions we take that give rise to the bad feelings. This requires self-critical observation, willpower, and perseverance. The easy way is to talk about how bored or hostile or depressed or helpless we feel and thereby derive momentary relief from our bad feelings. But in doing this, we entertain the misconception that we've done something to change our situation, or, more commonly, that we are not responsible for how we feel.

Feelings don't tell very much about who you are, but they do serve as good indicators of how you are faring on your journey through life. As diverse, erratic, and transient as feelings are, it is always possible to make an aggregate judgment about them as they arise over a period of time. For example, the people who come to see me can truthfully say (as they do), "Ed, I'm just not feeling good about myself," and their statement means something. (I've never yet had anyone come to me and say, "Gee, I'm feeling just great about life, can you help me make things worse?") It doesn't mean that these people have no happy emotions, any more than it means that strong, stable people don't encounter real "downs." But it does mean unmistakably that they are living their lives in such a way that their alarm system is chronically ringing. For something so major, dialogue and communication—the verbal manipulation, exploration, and analysis of feelings—will effect no lasting remedy. Only the alteration of the person's living habits can do that.

Thus feelings are most useful as sources of information about the personal satisfaction or dissatisfaction we are gaining from our long-range patterns of behavior and interaction. Beyond this function, however, feelings are frankly something to be somewhat wary of—not afraid of, and certainly not suppressed, but rather treated with humor and distance. Feelings, contrary to what we are led to believe these days, must not be permitted to become our sole preoccupation. In and of themselves, feelings don't have the dependability and depth to serve as our life's center. Feelings, in the realm of heart and spirit, are equivalent to opinion, in the realm of reason. They are common, changing, fickle, manipulable, superficial.

"But feelings are definitive!" remonstrate the growth experts. "Only when I share my feelings in gut-level communication am I truly sharing myself. It is true that my values, beliefs, and goals are more important than my feelings, but only when I tell you how I feel about my values, beliefs, and goals will you be able to perceive my uniqueness."[1] I'm afraid a person's life is not so simple as that; its uniqueness cannot be reduced to emotion or that life would be as unremarkable as the next, like refrigerators tumbling off an assembly line. Feelings are common. Actions in fulfillment of one's "values, beliefs, and goals"—or in fulfillment of love, work, the raising of children, one's faith—alone determine a person's

84

uniqueness. What I tell my lover about how I'm feeling just now carries about as much weight, therefore, as my informing her that I'm hungry or sleepy or horny.

"But feelings affect your love for your lover!" comes the reply of the latter-day love doctors. "When I tell you my emotions or feelings, I am telling you who I really am, I am giving you myself. . . Only when I share with you the many feelings that my love stirs in me will you be able to see my love as unique and unrepeatable."[2] Happily, for the sake of love—for its endurance and depth—this is not true. While love indeed arouses feelings, both pleasurable and painful, *feelings do not create love*. At the risk of setting off fits of apoplexy for a fifty-mile radius around the Esalen Institute at Big Sur, I have to say that your feelings about a loved one matter only as indicators of how well (or poorly) you're loving. The nature and purpose of love have little to do with feelings. Your love generates many things—joy, confidence, knowledge, ecstasy—that weigh in far heavier than feelings (as nice as they may be) on the scales of life. If your love were measured mainly in your own or your lover's feelings, what a sorry, superficial, undependable thing love would be. Feelings are conflicting, capricious, and very ordinary, somewhat like appetites in their monopoly of our consciousness. What is vital for you and your lover to experience, therefore, is not "the many feelings that my love stirs in me" (which run a gamut only from A to B), but rather the abiding patterns of action and interaction, of things you do together and alone, that your love generates.

In sum, feelings, and the communication of them, have been vastly overvalued by a culture that seeks deer in the garden of our shallow, passing emotions, if we experiment with sex and hone our techniques, if we undergo therapy that

85

explores the primordial unconscious springs of our feelings, then we can be spared the need for doing anything at all to change the way we live. This is simply not true.

Feelings are always with us, to be sure, and we must live with them, preferably controlling them, but occasionally falling under their domination for limited periods of time. When we do succumb to them, however, we should not endow them with more meaning and value than they have. For if we reduce the value of life to the inflated currency of feelings, then we are drastically cheapening ourselves and the human adventure. If we draft our wills, minds, and spirits into the service of feelings—and then judge them on how well they serve these little tyrants—we will truly have placed the cart before the horse. Actions, goals, beliefs, principles, love, faith—these things *in themselves* (and *not* how we feel about them) are the denominators, the definers of the uniqueness of our lives.

The apostles of "letting it all hang out" are as numerous today as hair-tonic salesmen were in the nineteenth century. One of the most successful is the Reverend John Powell, S.J., whose *Why Am I Afraid to Tell You Who I Am?* has sold in excess of one million copies. In his book *The Secret of Staying in Love*,[3] Father Powell writes:

> To see our way clear to this commitment of total honesty, we must face the fact that the only alternative to sharing in dialogue is somehow to "act out" these negative feelings . . .

> Secondly, we must be convinced that the"friction" of negative emotions is not a bad sign at all, but rather a sign of health and vitality in a relationship. . . .

86

"So I'm angry," says the master of the dialogical art. "I'm angry because you were late. I well know that this anger is simply my reaction to the situation because of something in me. I also know that there are others, less scarred than I psychologically, who would react differently, maybe even sympathetically. But this is me at this moment in my life. I feel angry and even vindictive. I feel a vengeful urge to put you through some kind of frustration or inconvenience, to make you wait on a lonely street corner for me. Of course, I won't do this. My emotions don't make my decisions for me. However, I just wanted you to know that this is how I feel. I've got anger and vengeance in me, I guess, and I want you to know that because I want you to know me."

Before we examine more closely the severe limitations and deceptiveness of Powell's counsel, let us give the growth movement, of which Powell is an advocate, its due. Like all myths, the myth of the usefulness of "getting your feelings out" started life with some validity, coming, as it did, in overt opposition to the stifling Victorian conventions that suppressed and repressed feelings and appetites wholesale. When society tries to force people to live a make-believe inner and outer harmony based on rigid conventions of behavior, morality, religion, and etiquette, it is not surprising that eventually the lid will be blown off. For people who have endured years of socially-enforced subjection and self-denial, the verbal expression of negative feelings—*prefacing and accompanying, as they did, whole programs of actions aiming to alter the status quo*—is a healthy and progressive sign.

Talking about, or encountering, feelings and appetites is not, in itself, a bad thing. It is, indeed, a good thing *if* it is the first step in the direction of doing something about them. You have, as they say, "half the battle won." But what about the other half? The problem is endlessly analyzing and expressing feelings, and then exploring, manipulating, evoking, arousing, and toying with them (for example, in primal-scream therapy, classical psychoanalysis, gestalt therapy, psycho-drama, encounter groups) will never get you even to the field of the next battle, which is by far the larger and more important one. Carried on long enough in a culture that has marinated itself in the ethos of purely verbal "liberation," the effect of communicating about feelings becomes counterliberating because the talking replaces the doing.

Turning to Powell's advice to the bearers of negative feelings, I would therefore say right off, "No, dialogue is *not* the only, or even the best, alternative to 'acting out.' It is only the easiest. The best alternative is to change what you are doing that produces the bad feelings." Negative emotions are neither bad signs nor good signs in themselves; they are simply signs indicating that something needs to be *done*, and they become good or bad, healthy or harmful, depending on what you do about the cause of the feelings. In other words, your daily pattern of living has to be changed.

The long soliloquy that Powell puts in the mouth of his "master of the dialogical art" is an eloquent effusion of the philosophy of our times, promising nothing by way of effort, detachment, critical use of reason, self-giving, intended improvement, or anything else that has to do with building strength in an individual or in a relationship. Does anyone seriously believe that my telling you I have moments of "vengeance" and "vindictiveness" in my heart (who does not?) constitutes an important contribution to our mutual knowledge? Is the kind of couple-knowledge that undergirds permanent love as we have been discussing it in this book afforded as easily as all this chest-baring indicates? No, couple-knowledge is much harder to come by than that. It goes much deeper than just talking about one's emotional states.

The trouble lurking in this kind of "open-heart" surgery is that the confider will manipulate the confidee with his confidences. Talking to someone in the heat of emotions *about* those emotions may just be a way of letting off steam and of regaining self-control. But it is *more* likely to result in one person's getting *the other person* to alleviate his pain by delivering a sympathetic or reassuring response. There are better ways. One might instead tolerate the negative emotion until it passes; *then* discuss and evaluate the behavior that generated the bad feelings, rather than the feelings themselves.

If I am hurt because my lover looks lustfully at someone else, and I rush to inform him or her of the full dimensions and nature of my hurt, my doing so subtly places on him or her part of the responsibility for my hurt. It's a way of fishing for an artificial response to placate me. Very occasionally, dealing with strong negative feelings is necessary (as we'll discuss in the next chapter); but expressing *all* negative feelings as a matter of course becomes a dangerous game that can deceive the "players" (allowing them to imagine they are accomplishing something important), distract them (because it keeps them from doing something important), and permit them to manipulate one another.

One other practical point about giving vent to bad feelings: I have learned (in my personal life and in my

89

counseling) that talking about feelings provides only a marginal and passing remedy. I know that the pain of bitter emotions is hard to tolerate and that we long to share the burden with each other; but we cannot share very successfully in verbal revelations. Essentially, in talking, we attempt to create alternative good feelings to counter the bad ones that burden us. Conversation, of course, is a time-tested means of generating and magnifying feelings in people, and if you can manage to strike a responsive chord in the other person— particularly if he or she is the apparent source of your bad feelings (I say "apparent" because naturally you alone are the creator of your feelings)—then perhaps you can manage to squeeze out a measure of relief for yourself through talk. But it won't last long because the whole effort is jerry-built and artificial; and you'll likely have paid too great a price on your own and the other person's behalf. A sure sign of personal strength—admittedly rare in our culture—is the capacity to deal with one's emotions privately as best one can (see Step Two). To be honest, only the passing of time and the feelings resulting from new behavior can bring much relief. And even then, unless *you* change the behavior patterns that cause bad feelings, there will be no longlasting relief.

* * *

Communication doesn't have to be about only bad feelings to be a false friend to a love relationship. A favorite traditional pastime of lovers is talking about their relationship, encouraged, as always, by the great power of words to arouse the emotions. Indeed, in its own way, a rapturous conversation between lovers is not unlike sexual intercourse; they have in common the apparent self-revelation and sharing, the intermeshing of two beings, the intimacy and violent emotions. Among the sexually inexperienced, insecure, or repressed, conversation may well be a highly refined, developed substitute for sexual relations.

Here again I am running the decided risk of sounding like a kill-joy. Only a kill-joy, after all, would want to keep young lovers from exchanging their sweet nothings. I am not at all the confirmed cynic I may appear to be—would an unromatic man write his wife love notes and put them in her shoe? I am no more opposed to "soul-raps" than I am to sex; I simply want to make it clear that such things do not contribute to building permanent love nearly as much as they are reputed to do.

The risks you take with excessive indulgence in deep talks about your love and relationship are multifaceted. For one thing, a clear and present danger in young relationships is that verbal intercourse will build vastly unrealistic expectations on the part of the two would-be lovers. To spin out mutual reveries of what your relationship could and should be, or to analyze excessively what it already is, is to overlay it with doubts and expectations and undercut seriously its potential for spontaneous, unself-conscious growth in the reality of daily life and interaction. In a society already inebriated on a heady mix of Freudianism and "candor," the chances of overindulging in analysis of words, thoughts, feelings, and actions are quite high. It may feel good to do it, but you are not adding to the relationship, and you may be inhibiting its growth by engendering false "highs" that daily living cannot sustain. Also, new lovers often talk of intimacies, pleasures, and fantasies not yet accomplished, which then creates a fantasy of closeness not yet attained, but to which feelings respond. This can create an illusion of closeness, which the couple is not ready to handle physically; for increased physical intimacy increases stress. But without sufficient relational strength, which takes time to build, this stress will lead the couple to an inevitable fall.

"Well, at least we're learning a lot about each other," might be a reply to my objection. But not even this is nearly so profoundly true as you may imagine. For me to tell you all about my secret longings, hopes, weaknesses, needs, my previous affairs, my relationship with my parents, my mistakes and failures, is really to tell you rather less than my actions would tell you about me if we spent a few days together pruning the black nightshade, going to church, talking quietly about a film we saw, cooking sukiyaki, playing skittles, window-shopping, and spending some time with children. For one thing, in the course of normal conversation a lot of this historical and emotional material would come out (but in its proper perspective), and for another thing, a person's verbal self-exposé simply doesn't expose much of what is important for a lover to know—that is, what is important to the building of a strong relationship. "Who am I?" is not, oddly enough, a question to which a profound answer would be made verbally.

Ironically, what words alone might show you these days is how proficient I am in my articulation and yet how distant my understanding of self and world are from reality. Not surprisingly, our verbal society has been obliged to "up" the word ante to the point that superlatives are now so commonly employed as to be meaningless. Something is no longer "neat" (to use a slang word of the late fifties), it is "unbelievable" or "super" or "out of sight." If I wasn't "up" for doing something ten years ago, now there is "no way" that I'll do it. Where I might have said "yeah" or "maybe," I now hear myself evincing a solid "for sure" (or "fer sher"). There is no need to overstress this point. Language, in general, like money, becomes inflated, that's all. And we have barely indicated the overkill in the language of "love," where this four-letter word itself is abused to the point of utter nonsense. Love is often the core of our greatest insecurities and needs for fulfillment, so we pull out the verbal plugs to kindle or intensify the flame. But all we really do is douse it with *unrealistic* (hence unrealizable) *expectations*. At best, words—deliberately chosen and moderately spoken—transmit meanings that have only a notional value in reality. What grounds words—that is, reinforces and *makes good on them*—are actions. To that extent, therefore, actions should precede words in a relationship as pawns precede major and minor pieces in a chess opening. It may seem lackluster, but twenty or thirty moves later you'll end up with a far stronger board position than the "hot dog" who advanced his big pieces without support.

* * *

Nevertheless, there is a time when words may be called upon to good purpose. The preceding pages were necessary to show why we have held up conversation to Step Three. Steps One and Two were the pawns, so to speak. Now that you have them well advanced, let us consider the deployment of the minor pieces. While "communication" as we've learned it from the growth experts is usually unhelpful or even harmful, conversation and discussion can play vital roles in creating

93

permanent love. While "communication" arises out of our wish to satisfy appetites, jangle emotions, and accomplish action-work with mouth-power, conversation is quite different in origin, nature, function, and process.

Conversation may not be exactly a dying art, as pessimists believe, but it is certainly an increasingly poorly practiced one. This is partly attributable to the lamentable effects of endless television viewing on the socialization and intellectual formation of the young.[4] Children and adults have a lot less opportunity to talk meaningfully with one another than they used to have, not to mention less knowledge of what discussion or conversation can be, how conversations are made, and what skills are required to sustain them. In addition, the rapid-transit style of domestic life in general discourages the cause of conversation.

The kind of talk that builds strength will flow naturally from the shared activities and lives you create in Step One (and will be improved by the skills and efforts you provide from Step Two). Conversations presuppose (as well as provide) a lot more strength than communications. Most fundamentally they presuppose a life built on activities (alone and shared) that truly absorb a person's interest and employ his talents, energy, and commitment. This is the fund from which conversations will draw their content and derive their meaning. Conversations thus shoot like rockets from these activities and are fueled by the heat that the activities generate. Where communication was a gingerbread house confected from the power of words to sugar-coat the absence of shared strengthful activity, conversation requires that a couple already be active in the pursuit of Steps One and Two. Conversation presupposes enough personal and relational security on the part of the participants in a relationship that they can unhook their attention from themselves and their immediate emotional sustenance and physical gratification, and refocus it on people, activity, interests, and unfolding events in the world.

At the end of a long day, in the evening, Hester and I might sit and discuss a problem I am having structuring a chapter in a book I'm writing. The discussion will not lack in intensity, vitality, disagreement, importance, passion, or emotion, for that matter, but it will not focus primarily on self or relationship. This fact notwithstanding, such a discussion still reveals a lot more about who I am (for example, about my struggles as a writer) and will contribute a lot more to building our relationship (by anchoring it in ongoing events crucial to both of us) than if we spent the time once again exploring feelings, reaffirming our love, or watching television.

Does it sound like I am prodding you to engage in stilted discussions? I hope not, for that is not my intention. Almost by definition, a discussion that is forced, unnatural, or self-conscious is *not* conversation. (It is closer to being "communication.") Step Three is not intended to urge you to run out and have a long talk with your lover about an article you've obliged yourself to wade through in the *Journal of Obscure Solecisms*. On the contrary, your conversation with your lover is (or should be) precisely the verbal outflow of what you normally do—be it reading the *Journal of Obscure Solecisms* or preparing for a tiddlywinks tourney. My Dad, at the end of a long day, would come home at night and always sit down with my Mom. Each with a mild drink in hand, they'd discuss the day's events for at least a half hour. We were welcome to join, and often we did. But as I reflect back, it was, to a great degree, their hour together before dinner.

Life in general—my life, your life, *any* life—is primarily

a material reality, and talking that forgets or distorts this fact quickly declines into mere "communication." Conversation, far more than "communication," remains faithful to (hence is supported by) the inscrutable, uncontrollable, unfolding *process* of two lovers' realities, for it flows from that reality rather than short-circuiting it in an attempt to strike directly at the emotions. Conversation tends to integrate two (or more) people into the reality of each other's lives and thereby deepen what they are (and do) together. Whereas communication masks reality or remains indifferent to it, conversation invites participation in life as well as in talk. Though conversation and communication both deal in words, and words are abstractions and idealizations, the words of conversation arise from and lead back to the stuff of life, whereas the words of communication tend often to be subtle means of idealizing, sugar-coating, romanticizing, manipulating. Thus it is best to create relaxing times to talk. Hester and I often talk in bed (a refuge from the children) or on our walks as we watch the beautiful Arizona sunsets or at a favorite restaurant by ourselves.

Nonetheless, I grant that Step Three—conversation— may seem stilted or unnatural to many people, regardless of the content of their talking, simply because they are not used to *any* conversation and have been leading lives of such impoverished activity (shared or individual) that they do not have a fund from which to draw. They are not used to concentrating on the "what" of talking. It cannot occur to them very readily that the substance of talk can be more important and more interesting than the emotional and psychological side effects and by-products. People who have never ridden horseback are going to find this activity initially uncomfortable, clumsy, and unnatural; but this fact does not in any way discredit this pursuit or detract from its advisability to people who initially might not enjoy doing it. Nevertheless, because conversation may be strained for many people who have been deprived of it, I have intentionally placed it third in the sequence of steps. Shared activity is less stress-provoking than conversation. Moreover, Steps One and Two will furnish the material from which fruitful hours of conversation will naturally emerge.

In sum, the art of conversation is a tributary of the art of loving. It can prove to be a major source of strength and confidence for a couple (and for a family as well). Conversation can finish the job that shared activity and individual effort have advanced by making what is implicit in the activity explicit to the human minds, spirits, and hearts involved. Conversation does its job when it makes for clarity, when it untangles and lays bare the meaning of the myriad of events, actions, transactions, thoughts, encounters that a couple may have experienced and shared in the course of a day, a year, or a lifetime. In conversation, a couple may lay claim, as it were, to the activity of their lives by understanding the meaning and course of that activity. Their conversation may also affect mightily the ways in which they act and interact by reallocating effort and redesigning a plan.

Conversation need not always be profound and serious; on the contrary, it may be, and often is, casual and humorous. It may address the playfulness in a relationship or a relationship's spiritual dimension (which we'll be discussing in the epilogue) as well as the more practical need of problem solving (Step Four). Conversation is a resilient plant and can grow in a number of natural climes—least satisfactorily, as we have seen, in a hot house; best under conditions of relaxation or in accompaniment to shared activity. Under conditions of too much emotion and conflict or of unrequited or inappropriate appetite, conversation is asked to carry too great a burden and tends to degenerate into frustration, game playing, and "communication." The exponents of communication would have us talk, touch, and gesture our ways through every impasse or turning—not a surprising outlook when you consider that the relationships founded on communication are themselves creations of words. But talk is not suitable to all occasions: It cannot resolve all problems or meet all needs. The predilection of our culture to overuse talk must be resisted. The couple in a strong relationship knows when to remain silent and when to disengage, verbally or otherwise, and when to trust the subliminal currents of shared activity either to remove the temporary obstacles or to reposition the lovers in a new time and place where conversation can prove more fruitful.

NOTES:

[1]John Powell, *The Secret of Staying in Love* (Niles, Ill.: Argus Communications, 1974), p. 78.

[2]Ibid.

[3]Ibid., pp. 145-147.

[4]See *For the Love of Children*, chap. 1.

STEP FOUR:

Working Out Difficulties
or
The Art of Compromise

We have brought ourselves to the point where we are sitting comfortably in our dens conversing agreeably with our lovers. And it would be nice if this book could end on so genial a note. The fact that it cannot (at least not yet) is a tribute to the challenge, uncontrollability, and fullness of life. Despite the best laid plans and most carefully taken steps, no love relationship, as no life, is immune to the periodic "slings and arrows of outrageous fortune." Indeed, for whatever crumb of consolation it affords us, the fact remains that it is through encountering and surmounting tragedy, upset, suffering, and conflict that human beings grow individually and in their relationships. Saint Augustine put the matter succinctly when he wrote that "The goodness of the world is not as great as the total of goodness and evil." In other words, the goodness that emerges out of the struggle with evil is greater than pure, pre-existing goodness. Angels may not agree; but for human beings, Augustine's insight reminds us of the incomparable value of confronting and transcending problems. You do not know the quality of your love for a person, or his for you, until you have met (and conquered) adversity together.

This chapter is written to help people develop the art of compromise in relationships, especially during times of stress. Every relationship will, from time to time, be beset by problems, major and minor, internal and external. External problems are those that happen outside of the relationship but have an effect upon it—the illness or death of a close relative or friend; your child's brush with the police and the courts; declining professional and financial fortunes. Internal difficulties arise within the relationship and may threaten to disrupt and destroy it—disagreements over the priorities of life; the stresses due to inequalities that develop between lovers over the course of years (such as professional success); sudden changes in the outlook or beliefs of one member of a relationship (such as a religious conversion). These examples may seem particularly grave, yet the likelihood is strong that most couples will have to deal with at least one of them (and probably more) in the course of their permanent love. Even if they do not, however, it is certain that they will face frequent challenges from minor stresses and problems. The practical advice this chapter provides will prove useful to all lovers dwelling this side of paradise.

Working out difficulties is mainly, as we shall shortly see, an aspect of talking, of conversation; but it also entails mutually shared activity and individual activity. It is, thus, something of a composite or synthesis of the previous steps of permanent love. Nonetheless, in itself, the ability to compromise constitutes the fourth step. It could not be dealt with any earlier than this, for, like Step Three (conversation), it very much presupposes the experience, confidence, and strength that accrue to lovers from successfully undertaking the first three steps on the path to permanent love. We noted earlier that problems cannot fruitfully be dealt with by lovers (or counselors) until there is strength in the bank. Indeed, many internal problems, including those resulting from a couple's inability to deal with major external problems, arise from a weakness in Steps One and Two. These problems, therefore, are only symptoms of the real problem. And this problem is invariably the same: the couple spends no time alone together; they have no time for building strength in their relationship. Thus, there is little or no residual strength, which the solving of problems presupposes.

Specifically, the strength needed by a couple if they are to weather the blasts of major stress, or the annoyance of chronic minor stress, is the couple-confidence that results from two lovers' experience at mutually solving problems. Presumably, any couple working on Step Four will have a track record of having done this by now, for much of the particulars of Step One will have turned out to entail the tandem dealing with a myriad of little challenges and difficulties. Planning a night out or a vacation, for example, will lead to planning a budget; playing monopoly will lead to working out the joint income tax. The joy and pleasure of doing small activities should not cover up the fact that these activities are creating the confidence and skill needed to accomplish the more difficult and stress-fraught tasks.

Confidence can come from play and leisure as surely as from serious problem-solving activity. If you have resolved between you the thorny question of where to put the roses and the cactus, or of how much space the vegetable patch should take up, then you are in a better position to allocate limited household funds and set financial priorities to the satisfaction of each. In sum, you have gained skill in compromise, flexibility, and responsibility. You will need to call on these, and much more, when serious problems arise.

Step Two will have made the vital contribution of teaching lovers how to work for their relationship on their own, how to be sensitive to the other's needs and flexible in their willingness to serve those needs. These qualities, plus the art and joy of conversation (Step Three), will all be mobilized when the weather turns stormy.

* * *

If I have seemed a bit alarmist or foreboding, like a man doing the hurricane watch on the beach at Galveston, it is because I know the force and bewildering suddenness with which problems can break unsuspectingly upon couples, swamping them in a torrent of negative emotions as well as seemingly overwhelming decisions, demands, and dilemmas. Great strength can be used up like a fat bank account when, for example, unexpected medical bills drop into a couple's life along with accident and illness. And neither the challenge nor the damage is merely external. The internal dynamics of even the stablest relationship can be thrown awry by the impact of a disfiguring illness or operation (such as a mastectomy or paralysis) or a psychologically "charged" medical procedure (such as an abortion or a vasectomy). A very stable newly-married couple came to me on the verge of dissolution because the previous day the man learned he had syphilis, and the woman would not believe he was faithful, which he was indeed. She had carried the disease from a previous premarital affair.

In another instance, I worked for a long time with a couple whose relationship was thrown into great turmoil by the powerful religious conversion of one partner and by the ensuing surprise, isolation, and resentment of the other. The relationship of yet another couple, who seemed to be doing very well over many years, collapsed completely when the woman had a third, unplanned-for child late in life. In short, the unfolding of life brings many crises and passages. Some, such as childbirth, death, menopause, aging, can be foreseen—though this does not seem to mitigate their intensity or difficulty—but others are entirely unexpected. No one can assume that oneself or one's relationship with another is strong enough to automatically weather any storm. "Fear and trembling," to borrow the Danish philosopher Kierkegaard's phrase, is sometimes the most realistic frame of mind in which to contemplate the possibilities of fate— though I would add "hope," as well.

Presently I shall be delineating a four-stage process for couples to use in working out major difficulties. It presupposes, however, (in addition to the strength derived from Steps One through Three) a measure of detachment from, or a willingness to tolerate the pain of, emotion. I realize that such detachment may be hard to come by in the midst of a large problem's sudden explosion on the scene—or in the midst of the momentary upsurge of strong emotions attending a familiar problem (if the problem is more long-term and chronic). The point is, emotion offers no help in working out difficulties. Having a long, candid discussion with your partner about the way you're feeling, or even just informing him of your feelings, is *not* (in my opinion) a sound approach to problem solving. I realize that many counselors disagree with me about this, but I stand on my experience with people. If revelations about feelings are ever in order (an arguable point), the time for revelation would be long after they have subsided, not while they are being experienced. Feelings are too uncontrollable, too liable to lead to manipulation of both parties, too volatile to serve as the basis for working out a problem.

Working out the difficulty, therefore, will be *the couple's assignment*. To contain and work through profound (negative) emotions preceding the problem solving is *the personal business of the emotional one(s)*. So say something like, "Look, honey, I'm upset right now, but I'll calm down eventually, and when I do, we'll deal with the problem together." Then go off by yourself, or do whatever feels best as a means of tranquilizing your emotions. (Solitude is a valuable resource here, but most people cannot handle inactive solitude, and they should *do* something while they're alone—perhaps a light, undemanding activity that produces good feelings, such as a run, a swim, a hot bath, a rest.)

If your partner is the one experiencing the emotions, leave him alone. This may be hard to do, particularly if you're feeling especially critical, as you may well be at the moment. Your intervention now—even if it is benign and benevolent—won't help as much as your supportive

106

disengagement. (Any comment may sound critical and thus increase the problem.) *You have to trust your partner's self-confrontation, the unfolding of his inner process*. The strength that you'll need to do this comes from your own achievement of Step Two, where you learned to trust your own inner process. If you've been working hard at developing your personal powers of working through, of self-examination, of sensitivity to other people's needs, of dealing with emotion, then you will know precisely what your partner is going through now and why he needs space apart—freedom. He must do what he has to do by himself, or he'll never be in a position of strength to proceed to the problem solving with you later on.

One final warning: late afternoon, when the several members of the household return home from the day's activities, is a highly charged, vulnerable time. I call it "the crisis hour," and it may run anywhere (depending on your schedules) from four to seven p.m. The end of the day is a time of transition between two very different kinds of activity—work and leisure. Many different kinds of stress may surface. There is the obvious factor of fatigue and tension after a day at the office, or in school, or at home with children or housework. But a person also needs time to prepare himself for a new set of stimuli and the new demands that result from these stimuli. This is a time for unwinding, moving from one kind of high (or low, depending on the sort of day it has been) to a position of openness and receptivity to another, very different kind. The transition takes awhile to occur, and during this time a person needs space and quietness. He has internal gears to shift and weariness to recover from. The time is not propitious for intense conversation or demanding activity.

I had a couple come to see me because they were "fighting a lot." As it turned out, the time when their worst skirmishes took place was late in the afternoon when the husband, Joe, came home from work. His young wife, Anne, put the baby promptly in his arms the moment he walked into the house so that she could make dinner while "you play with our son awhile; I've had him all day." Now Joe is a loving father; but the tension of work had not subsided before he was confronted with the demand to play with an infant. He did so with animation, but the price paid was that he and Anne frequently started arguing over trifles before, during, and after dinner, and then the whole evening was ruined. Oddly enough, they never made the connection between their liability to squabbling and the need for time and space to unwind. (If people did make these connections, I'd be out of a job, I guess.)

When I spelled out what I saw as part of the problem, Anne remonstrated, "But, gee, I keep Brad all day long. Can't I have a rest from him when Joe comes home?" Fair question. In the tranquility of my office, away from the emotion of their home at twilight, we set ourselves to the task of working out Joe and Anne's difficulty. Eventually it was agreed that a neighbor lady and Anne would take turns spelling each other with their children during the day. This gave each her own time to relax. Meanwhile, their husbands took a half hour or forty-five minutes to unwind when they arrived home.

* * *

When the time (finally!) arrives to begin the process of working out difficulties, you needn't hire a brass band to play a fanfare. But nonetheless, the moment should be designated and accepted as "consecrated" by both lovers. In other words, the process should not be an off-the-cuff sort of transaction sandwiched in between phone calls, children, and sundry distractions. This only augments the chance that emotions and conflict will reerupt and send both players back to square one. It is equally vital that *both* parties work on resolving difficulties, major or minor. Step Two of permanent love permits lovers to do many things on their own; but working out mutual difficulties is *not* one of them. The big risk that is run if one party constantly carries the heavier burden in the resolution of problems is that individual self-confidence may result but at the expense of couple-confidence; and eventually the resentment builds up in both parties (the one saying, "Why should I always be the one to solve the problems and concede ground?"; the other saying, "How come I never have a say in what goes on around here?").

The first stage of the process is for both parties to *identify* (to their mutual agreement) *the problem* as specifically as possible. When this is accomplished, each party should then take a close look at how he or she is contributing to the problem. If, as often happens, it turns out there are several problems troubling the partners, then they should separate them out and attend to them one at a time, starting with the easiest. (The easier ones are stressful enough, and in solving them, the bigger ones often disappear.)

The key to this initial stage is to make sure each lover *describes only his own behavior, without making comments or offering observations about the behavior of the partner.* This might prove very difficult to one partner when he or she is convinced the other is hiding or distorting or neglecting an aspect of his behavior that seems to strongly contribute to the problem. It is best, however, *even in this instance*, for each partner to remain steadfastly on his own turf and say nothing provocative. Here again Step Two comes into play—*trusting in the partner's inner process*, which, even though he may temporarily fudge a bit in the self-criticism department, will very likely lead him eventually to contribute his full share in resolving the problem. (And once he has done his share, which he may proceed to do silently, don't bring it up—don't indulge the need to glory in scoring a point.)

I remember a humorous story of one young couple. The problem we were working on concerned each partner's spendthrift habits. Both worked, and both spent more than they earned. When their negative feelings abated, and we hunkered down to stage one in the process of working out difficulties, neither partner exactly distinguished himself by the exhaustiveness of his account of his own expenditures. (In fact, I was reminded of the routine reports posted publicly by congressmen and senators of their personal finances.) I chided the two for how little they had to say now that the rules of the game forbade comments about the other person's spending.

What was important was not that each partner perfected his style of public confession but rather that each agreed, if falteringly, to at least begin the process of inspecting his own behavior. The very experience of even a little bit of this kind of self-revealing candor is vital; it sows the seed for future self-critical examination.

In stage two, the partners *evaluate*[1] *the behavior they have identified in stage one*. We know now what we're both doing. What behaviors are helping and can be built upon? What are we doing that needs to be changed?

In answering these questions, lovers will have to resist two related temptations: (1) the need to hash over endlessly "what went wrong," and (2) the need to castigate themselves, individually or collectively, for the "failure" that led to these difficulties. I am not saying that something didn't, in fact, go wrong, nor that someone didn't, in truth, fail. I am saying only that there is a much greater likelihood that people will grow from their failures if they don't dwell on them morbidly. Similarly, I am not opposed to long discussions and profound reflections on the past, but let it be on past successes. I sincerely agree with Santayana that by understanding their past (both individually and collectively) people may perhaps avoid repeating some of their mistakes. *But* detailed historical analysis of failure has no place in the process of working out difficulties; the strong accent must be placed on present and future. Again, you can build a strong present only on past successes, not past failures.

By the way, it shouldn't be surprising to learn that feelings play a major, obscuring role in this obsession with the past. Bad or guilty feelings will certainly have arisen in the wake of weak behavior, and those feelings will want to assuage themselves any way they can—by outbursts of words, self-hatred, blame-throwing, excessive in-depth analysis. But the feelings themselves are not useful to the lovers or the counselor, both of whom are concerned with working out difficulties and *altering behavior*. Feelings have to be accepted, of course, and soothed when they are too painful. But they must not be permitted to direct the course of the therapeutic session. The feelings are certain to serve as constant reminders that we have screwed up; but only the operation of mind and will can effect useful antidotes and solutions. Again, behavior causes feelings, not the reverse. *Also, I do not believe that*

111

unhappy feelings arising from past failures or episodes will in any way affect a present relationship if there are sufficient, enjoyable strength-building activities in the present (lots of Steps One, Two, and Three). Only present miseries will reinforce past unhappiness.

Dwelling on "what went wrong," offers no solutions to the problem at hand. Instead it mires the couple in excuses. Too much asking "Why?" doesn't lead to a solution: it excuses us from *seeking* a solution. Instead of working, we talk, and our irresponsibility grows. I may really have a bad temper. My wife may very well nag. We both may be tired, hot, and upset. All these may well be valid excuses. But they skirt the problem, and making excuses—even valid excuses—*gives the illusion* that the problem is being solved when it isn't. How we should alter the pattern of our living in the future is the question that needs to be faced.

Thus, in stage two, you must make a brisk evaluation of the behavior you've identified in stage one. What is there that can be built upon contructively, and what is there that plainly requires change? The former question will bring to light the good that you have done; the latter will require mutual *creative* work from both lovers for additional, constructive alternatives.

Stage three entails *spelling out specific alternative behavior.* You both agree on what the problem is; it is clear that certain changes must be effected. But *how are these changes to take place?* Let the ideas flow from both of you freely and noncritically. Make a list if necessary, but do not exclude any alternative before examining it. If irritation disrupts the process here (or at any stage in the process), then "let go" and recommence at some other time when emotions have ebbed. In this stage you will be mobilizing your intellectual resources—just you and your lover combining forces to surmount another of life's difficulties. This is where you will have the chance to distinguish yourselves as a resourceful team able to "serve each other wittily in the tangle of your minds" (if I may quote Sir Thomas More in *A Man for All Seasons*). The plans and alternatives you devise will be what determine how effectively you solve the difficulty and insure that it does not recur.

I still remember Alice and Jim. It took them ten minutes to climb the short staircase to my office. Alice had been one of the four million Americans who were seriously injured in car accidents that year. She had lost the use of one leg, and the other was impaired in its functioning. With crutches and Jim's assistance, she could painfully and slowly make herself marginally ambulatory. Their problem was, not surprisingly, that until the accident they had been a very active couple. Much of the content of their Step One (shared activity) had focused on physical activity—sports, physical recreation, playing with their children, and so on. Now, very suddenly and very tragically, the shared ground of their interaction, their love, would have to change.

Not especially verbal or intellectual people, Alice and Jim came to me with the complaint (symptom) that "we are bickering a lot more now than ever before." I must confess that I felt considerable admiration for the strength of their union that a disaster such as the one that had befallen them had brought on no greater dislocations than "we bicker more than we used to." Talking to them was easy. They were eager for understanding. The two loved each other greatly and were utterly committed to their marriage. They were profoundly accustomed to working at Steps One, Two, and (to a lesser extent) Three of permanent love. It took no time for them to see the underlying cause of the "bickering." The problem was thus specific: how to grapple with the new situation created by Alice's handicap.

Just because a problem is specific, however, does not mean it is easy to resolve. I have seen many couples dissolve their union in the face of far smaller odds than the ones facing Alice and Jim. What would be needed here, besides large measures of courage and fortitude (which they were plainly showing), was applied intelligence to devise means of building a new life as similar as possible to the old life that had given them such strength and pleasure.

My first question to them, therefore, after we had briefly delineated the problem and its origin, was this: "All right, what can you do together now?" They began to run down a long list of what they used to do but could no longer do because of Alice's condition. I cut them off and repeated my request: "I didn't ask what you can't do, I asked what you *can* do." A long pause followed, and you could literally (from their faces) watch their brains shift gears (from reverse to forward). Slowly their minds—working separately at first, then combined—began to grind out answers to the question.

At first the answers were hesitant and uninspired: "We can play cards, go for a drive, read to each other. . ." I did not supply them with more; they would have to find these on their own, or they would not succeed as a couple in their life ahead. Alice and Jim went home from this first session with a small list of pretty lackluster alternatives, and they came back the following week very impatient to find newer, more satisfying answers to their problems. The vexing question of how to go about laying the foundations of a new life hovered over them.

Gradually their alternatives, suggestions, and plans began to reflect the large stature of the people who were Jim and Alice. The first major step forward came when the two of

114

them found a way for Alice to recover the sense of self-worth she had lost when she quit her job (which she had been obliged to do in the wake of the accident). Always something of an amateur artist, Alice now concentrated on developing her interest and skill in that area, and soon she began to design greeting cards that she sold from her home. Jim helped her write the messages inside, and slowly this became a respectable little business.

But this was only the first of an almost endless series of difficult steps. The couple had to use their resources to solve all manner of problems, from restructuring their sex life to restructuring the pedals of their automobile so that Alice could drive. Jim had to learn when, and when not, to assist his wife so as to help her without making her childlike or dependent; Alice had to accustom herself to physical therapy and the use of accessories; the two of them had to learn how, and when, to talk about the accident and Alice's new life situation. They spent a great deal of time and effort finding satisfying substitutes for the tennis, running, and skiing they had loved and done so well. They took up swimming, table tennis, and archery; and they became avid spectators at tennis matches and equestrian shows.

In short, Alice and Jim had the choice either of making creative use of their pooled resources to find ways of solving their "problem," or of abandoning the love relationship that had brought them both such strength and happiness for so many years. It came down to how successful they would be in rebuilding what seemed to be a thoroughly broken life together. *They* were successful; many others aren't. The important factor here, courage aside, was the mutual skill and effort that Alice and Jim put into devising creative solutions to tough problems.

The fourth and final stage in the art of compromising is really an adjunct to the third: *review and reevaluate the plan you made and are carrying out*. Try it faithfully for a period of time, but then review it as necessary. In the case of Jim and Alice, plans were constantly reformulated to be more beneficial. It is important for couples to progress at their own speed. Plans must reflect the *mutual* ability and willingness of the lovers and not the audacity or timorousness of either of them. Thus, as time passes and the lovers grow, plans need to reflect the changes that have been wrought. The reason I have bothered to make reviewing and reevaluating a separate stage in the process is that many couples do one of two things once they have devised a plan: either they serve the plan as if it were God incarnate or, once their life begins to improve, they stop working at their plan. It is always amazing to me how couples, once their life has improved, stop doing the very thing which made them happy. It's like starting a car engine, driving out on the freeway, and then turning the motor off and expecting the car to keep on going.

Most difficulties don't go away easily. Even if they appear to, the long-term carrying through of a periodically reviewed and updated plan not only will deal effectively with the specific difficulty in question but also will put the couple in the habit of self-observation and mutual effort, which will help them in dealing with all problems that arise. One couple I counseled decided to have a regular Sunday-night review (in this case the couple taught the counselor) by checking their plan in two areas: first, identifying what they had done the past week that was enjoyable and, second, deciding what new activity they might try the following week. They made no mention of fault or failure. And working together on a plan—both in what it includes and excludes—is the real crux of strength-building. For it leads to the internal recognition that we are capable of finding better ways to live our life. This is what permanent love is all about.

NOTES:

[1]I purposely used the word, *evaluate* instead of *judge*, as I have previously used terms like *dysfunctional* or *weak* instead of *evil* and *wrong*. Now is as good a time as any to say why.

Let me say at the start, I do not approve of contemporary philosophies or methodologies which attempt to wipe away or paper over the profound, ineradicable spiritual and moral dimensions of human life. In a word, I find the attempt immoral, even sinful, and I have not a twinge of hesitation to put it thus.

However, because I do attach meaning to the categories of the moral and the spiritual, I think it is essential that we give them more than lip-service. Precisely because *sin* and *evil* do have very real significance, in other words, we must find ways of transmitting what we mean by those words to generations of people who conceive of *sin* and *evil* in the archaic, distorted, ritualized ways which traditional culture and religious institutions have disseminated. What the behavioral sciences have provided is not, therefore, a means of eluding the tragic vision of life, or the spirituality of man, or the conflict of good and evil, but rather a vocabulary and approach which permit us to communicate these old meanings in new, possibly more effective ways.

I had a couple come to me who had been raised strictly in the old (pre-Vatican II) Roman Catholic Church. Dauntless and unremitting in their religious practice and adoption of Church vocabulary, they showed an all-but-invincible predisposition toward stigmatizing many of their thoughts, words, and actions with judgments like *sinful* or *evil*. Doing so, however, never seemed to help. Never before or since have I sat in my armchair and listened to two people more hell- or heaven-bent on anathematizing themselves, each other, and everyone else, but rarely before or since

117

have I seen a case where all the pious sound and fury signified so little in terms of *doing* anything differently.

If a counselor could get this (or any similar) couple to step back from their inveighing long enough to cast a calm, criticial, but *nonjudgmental* eye on their situation, he might lead these people to render action-service, not just lip-service, to the faith and morals that so visibly animated them. Once again the paradox of momentarily "letting go of something (that is, a traditional vocabulary) in order to better possess it" comes into play. If we can make use, for clinical and therapeutic purposes, of less highly charged terms and concepts like "evaluation," "dysfunction," "noncritical," "emphasize the positive," "deemphasize the negative," and so on, *without thereby wishing or claiming to ban the moral and spiritual dimensions of life*, then we might better serve these very religious and ethical principles than if we continued to mouth the traditional words in the traditional ways.

Beyond Human Love

Oh God make me brave.
Let me strengthen after pain
As a tree strengthens after rain,
Shining and lovely again.

As the blown grass lifts, let me rise
From sorrow with quiet eyes,
Knowing Thy way is wise,
God make me brave.

Life brings such blinding things!
Help me to keep Thee in sight,
Knowing all through my night,
That out of dark, comes Light.

Dorothy Brandt Ford

We are approaching the end of the journey that we have taken together. It has not been a long trip, but I hope you have seen some new countryside and, more importantly, taken a different look at what you thought to be familiar ground. The challenge and joy of love and our need for love have not diminished; only our capacity to practice loving has become impaired for reasons we have already discussed. The problem with romantic love, or Eros, is not that it is a great and powerful love. No love need trouble us simply because it is strong. On the contrary, as a general rule of thumb, the surest sign of strength in a human being is the amplitude of his love.

The problem with romantic love is threefold: first, we as a society have fundamentally distorted romantic love and its practice; second, we have attended disproportionately (nearly obsessively) to our distorted notion of romantic love in contrast to the feeble effort we invest in other, equally important, forms of loving; and third, we have permitted our version of romantic love to exert a baneful influence on all our forms of loving. Thus, throughout this book I have focused attention fairly constantly on romantic love, but in somewhat the same fashion that an exorcist concentrates on the possessed—not from attraction, but by necessity. The urgent need is to reintegrate the bedeviled one back into the world of which he was a part—humanity at large, loving in general. As the exorcist must dispel myth, illusion, demonical selfishness, I have tried to cut through the mystification and fantasy that have taken control of our erotic lives and destroyed so many of our love relationships.

The purpose, then, of the steps toward permanent love has been mainly *practical* and *restorative*. These steps are intended to lead us back to understanding and practicing romantic love as an activity of the will, not as a projection of the feelings. But the emphasis lies on the doing. A theoretical analysis, no matter how trenchant, is only the first small step. Words alone are already part of the problem, as we have seen. Shortcuts, exceptional analyses, new psychotherapies, weekend dithers, novel interpersonal techniques, and so forth, are distinctly *not* what we need more of. Philosophers have interpreted the world, noted Karl Marx, but *the point is to change it*. The unique justification for another book on love, therefore, is that it might lay out a path for people to follow in order to change. If my method has seemed lackluster, repetitive, single-minded, and businesslike, that is intentional. Calm, clear exposition that recalls the daily, active, intentional, continuous, unexceptional, mundane qualities of *all* love, romantic love especially, is what we need and what I have tried to furnish.

The steps, in other words, are not new, but old—very old. They only seem new because we as a society have a short, selective memory. These steps will help you realign your loving with your living. And they will show you that although we are all sentient creatures, we are *first* purposive, willful creator-creatures. Were it not thus, I doubt we would have survived as long as we have. And were we not to recall and reclaim this quality, I doubt we would long survive. Particularly the first two steps accent the vital necessity of applied effort in constructing long-term love relationships. There is no magic; there is—more importantly—the couple knowledge and couple confidence that come from shared activity, preferably goal-oriented, resource-mobilizing activity. There is no magic; there is—more importantly—the personal self-reliance and selflessness that result from time alone for concentration on one's own responsibility and growth in a relationship.

If by now you don't "understand" what I am saying, it's not because my ideas are complex; it's because you aren't willing to work. And fair enough. Many people are not. Life will teach them, not that I am right, but that they are misguided in looking for panaceas and gimmicks in an area where life permits no short-circuitry or jaywalking.

If, however, you do accept the fundamental thesis on which this book is hinged, then the time has come to take stock of where we are now that we have left Step Four behind. And the first thing to say is that Steps One through Four are *not* behind but *beside* us. The activity of loving is ongoing. You cannot store it up like profits or capital that can then be spent when the activity has ceased. The activity of loving is more like staying in shape physically. You have to keep doing it all your life. You may have the reassurance of knowing that your body can sustain you through periods of illness or forced inactivity; but sooner or later (preferably sooner) you'll have to recommence your running or swimming (or whatever you do to stay in condition). Similarly with the steps toward permanent love, the strength they afford is cumulative only as long as you keep doing them. The bad news, in other words, is that there is no respite (for long); but, as you know by now if you're doing the steps, the *very* good news is that once you get into the habit of sharing strength-building activity with loved ones and working at your own contribution to your relationships, then you won't want to slide back to the narcissism and sloth of what passes for love in a lovesick society.

You will also have discovered by now that the steps really do apply to *all* varieties of love, not simply to romantic love, even though (for reasons stated at the outset) we framed our discussion and selected our examples in terms of Eros. By

124

linking romantic love with the activity of a full life, how could we not have formulated steps that did not apply universally? More to the point, in demystifying romantic love, how could we have avoided showing that Eros is not all there is to love, or that it is not fundamentally different from other kinds of love? Love, as an activity (or *the* activity) of the soul, is unified, despite its varied manifestations, just as reason, *the* activity of the mind, is essentially one capability with many applications and purposes. Romantic love only seemed different to us because we made it a creature of the emotions, of the appetites, and of fantasy, because it became so divorced from the intentionality, responsibility, unexceptionality, and quiet joy that mark our practice of all "will-full" activities.

Step Two contains a paradox that flies directly in the face of today's notion of love: in certain basic ways, it doesn't matter *whom* you love, but *how* you love. Moreover, not only is the identity of your love objects somewhat irrelevant, but how much they love you is also not *fundamentally* critical to your own growth as a lover. Note that I am not saying we don't *need* people in our lives. We do; but we need them more to show our own love than to receive theirs (as much as we need that, too). The familiar letting-go-in-order-to-hang-on paradox returns again at this point: The more we concentrate on loving, the more we become lovable ourselves—and as day follows night, the more we become loved. But the first priority is to love selflessly and unconditionally; and only then will self be served.[1]

* * *

125

As we progress along the path toward permanent love, it is curious to note how the challenges and demands as well as the joys and satisfactions of love in all its faces rise to meet our expanded capabilities. The Peter Principle does not apply to loving. There is no way we can be "promoted" beyond our capacity to love, for that capacity is unceasing. Love accepts no final plea of "incompetence" any more than it dispenses a verdict of "complete competence." Love is always "in session," from the time we become capable of loving (around our eighth or ninth birthday) to the time we die. Where there is the challenge of living, there is the challenge of loving.

This book, from start to finish, was written by and for people who, implicitly or explicitly, have accepted life's challenge (and love's requirement) to continually struggle to improve their capability to love. Though each of us grows in his unique, appointed way, there are common elements and benchmarks in the development. We have reached a point now (after Step Four) where it is possible to consider some of love's later, higher challenges and demands. It is not that we had no idea of them before this point, nor even that they weren't softly present in the moments of our finer loving. It is, rather, that the strength they require of us in exchange for the awesome strength that they bestow, was not ours to give until we had drunk deeply and fillingly of love.

If the steps (particularly Step Two) have taught us anything, it is to appreciate our own and each other's bottomless capacity to be human—that is, to do the unpredictable, the irritating, the unloving, the inconsiderate, as well as the selfless, the affectionate, the transcendent, and the intelligent. Our development in love, as we have already noted, brings ample confrontation with the pain and stress of relationships, as well as with their pleasure and joy. As infants, we revel in the fountain of love pouring from our parents; but early on we have to learn about and to accomodate the tension and anxiety created by limits, separation, discipline. As children, we prize the wonderful abandon and intensity of our first friendships, but we are also obliged to tolerate hurt feelings, disappointments, and loss when our young friends act like unfeeling, self-centered boobs—that is, like people.

As teenagers and young adults, we encounter the magnetism of romantic love, which absorbs our attention and energy, easily dispensing ecstasy and despair with cavalier indifference to our wishes and emotions. This early encounter with romantic love teaches us sooner and quicker than any other love the power of love to establish its own law in our lives. As C. S. Lewis noted, in romantic love we have "a religion of our own, our own god. Where a true Eros is present, resistance to his commands feels like apostasy, and what are really . . . temptations speak with the voice of duties—quasi-religious duties, acts of pious zeal to love. He builds his own religion around the lovers."[2] Whatever the fickle or questionable nature of the early erotic motivation, the fact remains that romantic love provides many people's first major lesson in the need for self-giving and altruism in love.

That lesson is directly built upon when, in early adulthood, we encounter what ought to be maturer forms of romantic loving, where our will replaces our emotions, appetites, and fantasies as the principle controlling agent of loving. It is essential that the will (and through the will, reason and spirit) take a position of ascendance in Eros because the demands of mature romantic love for selflessness, patience, growth with another can never be enduringly or

127

satisfactorily met by the fulfillment of emotions and fantasies. Once the will becomes active, charity in love becomes possible (and I'm speaking now of charity in the religious sense of disinterested, or selfless, giving). And charity in love is necessary, particularly once a "courtship" phase has passed and the lovers are settling down to interweave their lives.

The need for charity in loving grows even greater with the advent of children in one's love relationship. With one's mate, giving bears at least some semblance of mutuality. But with children, especially in infancy and early childhood, the loving is nearly a one-way street. Even in puberty and adolescence, a young person's responsive giving to his parents will be a lot more tempered, ambivalent, and thoughtless than a selfish parent might want. Yet the need for the parents' unconditional love remains.

The challenges of living and loving climb yet another notch for people moving into late middle age. Even granting the strength that comes from long-term fulfillment of Steps One through Four on the path toward permanent love, the challenges of aging—the need to restructure the conjugal relationship now that children are gone; the inexorable arrival of sickness, physical suffering, perhaps disfigurement or impairment; the swath cut by death among loved ones; the threat of death to one's own life—require a personal and mutual strength that Steps One and Two, by themselves, do not provide. An element of charity has been advisable all along in our loving, but it now becomes the cornerstone of strength and joy.

* * *

I remember distinctly Ron and Betty's first visit, because I don't usually get very many clients in their late fifties. I call them clients, but actually they bore very slight resemblance to ninety-nine percent of the people I work with, and, in truth, they had come to see me "for a chat" on the advice of close friends we have in common. Ron was a distinguished attorney in our community and Betty was equally well known for her charitable, religious, and cultural work. As they spoke about their marital relationship and their relationships with others, I sensed nothing obviously wrong. The patterns of their lives interwove with a completeness that was enviable; their children were grown and doing well (though living far from home); they both maintained longstanding friendships that brought them pleasure and diversion; both of them seemed to enjoy their work. The checklist of areas of strength and weakness (in terms of love and worth) that I always run down in my mind in the first session with new clients gave no obvious clues to any missing strengths. I was left with only my vague impression of a distant tension between nearly complacent self-satisfaction and assurance, on the one hand, and a semiconscious anxiety or longing on the other. The two of them, particularly Betty, spoke often of sickness and death—several close friends of theirs having lately been claimed by these eventualities. At the end of the hour, however, I could not really see where our chat had led us.

Betty called me about a week later and said she was coming to see me alone. "We came together last week," she told me upon entering my office, "but Ron came along only for my sake. I'm sure he doesn't believe we need to see a counselor. I'm not sure we need to either. But I do feel like talking to someone. . . I'm not even sure about what." In her husband's absence, the woman had fewer inhibitions about delving beneath the exterior of her feelings and thoughts about her life. "I love my children very much," she said at one point (she had five grown ones—four married, and three with children of their own), "but I don't understand them." The last phrase was spoken with an edge of bitterness that I had detected before in Betty's voice. I asked her what she meant by "don't understand them."

It turned out that Betty resented the fact that her children viewed love and marriage so differently from the way she did. She had invested by far the better part of thirty-five years into raising them. Now, however, they showed no inclination to want large families of their own, nor to spend the same kind (or amount) of time raising children as their mother had done. Moreover, although they all seemed dutiful and authentic in their desire to visit their parents, Betty was not fully satisfied with the frequency of her children's trips home or their attention to her. "I know I'm expecting too much," she said, "but somehow I can't stop myself from doing so."

As we spoke, the conversation touched other areas. Betty's feelings about her husband also betrayed underlying unrealistic expectations, a diffuse bitterness that the expectations were unmet, and guilt when she confronted the bitterness. Betty held similar feelings concerning her religious practice. She was entirely discontented with the new rector, though she admitted that she "couldn't really say why." Closer questioning brought to light the very unremarkable statement (familiar to any counselor who has worked with religious people and clergy): "I sometimes think this whole religion thing is a big farce anyhow. I really wonder if God cares a damn about us." There followed a long tirade against the hypocrisy of the church; against the lack of charity among the clergy; against the uselessness of parochial schools ("What good did it do to send our kids there? I don't see them acting any differently from other children in their generation."); and against the lack of "inner support" that she expected her steadfast religious practice to provide.

Interlaced in this rapidly spoken monologue were frequent references to "getting older," to the sickness and death of close friends. She showed veiled concern about her own fading sexual attractiveness and the possibility of Ron's "running off with some cutie-pie." And she felt unfulfilled by much of her public work: "The younger women can't wait for the people my age to retire from boards [of directors] so that they can take over." At the end of the session, she asked despairingly, "God, Ed, what's it all about anyway?"

* * *

Like Betty, many, many people of all ages give urgent voice to the never-ending frustrations of their unmet expectations, not just of romantic love, but of *all* human love. People experience this frustration even where strength is present, where responsibility and duty have been exercised, where the will is the center of the person, where appetites are not repressed, where love in its many aspects has been present, and where great disasters have not befallen the person. The need for understanding and charity, for unconditional giving and tolerance, for forgiveness and acceptance, seems to grow and grow, eventually outstripping what any of us can honestly be expected to provide on the basis of Step Two. It would be reassuring if the steps toward

131

permanent love could provide more than simply strength—if they could provide shields or immunity or omnipotence in the face of what life has to offer. But they cannot. Human love is simply not enough. There are too many Betty's working hard and succeeding at human love but failing nonetheless in the long haul because there was no spiritual strength underpinning, or crowning, their love.

The direction in which human love points is, ultimately, *only* a direction, not an achievement. The need for charity cannot be met by unaided human love. The insufficiency of human love to meet the trials and demands of life (and of loving) was a realization that came *from the experience of living and loving*. With the best of intentions, we formulated the four steps to permanent love; but in sincerity, and from the experience of trying to practice them, we have to conclude that they cannot work on their own.

In the last analysis, no person can be assured of achieving permanent love because by our very nature, we human beings are inconsistent in our actions. Love, if it is to be permanent in the face of all vicissitudes, must ultimately be grounded in the Source of Love. God's love for man (called agape) and man's reflection of that love in interpersonal relationships (charity) do indeed promise invincibility and permanence. But the fact that this is so does not mean that we are promised neat solutions or the absence of trial and tribulation. We are not talking now about the gods sometimes confected by organized religion or revival movements— especially the gods of religious routine or emotional frenzy. Betty's testimony sufficed to demolish the "strength" that they provide. Moreover, professed belief and regular religious practice must be founded on living faith and enacted beliefs, or it will not stand up in the hurricane-force winds that periodically and often unexpectedly blow across our paths. Just as our love for one another has slight meaning unless it is enacted over a long period of time, so our love for God and our acceptance of His love for us, will have no *reality* for us if we let it become routinized, trivialized with lip-service, distorted by emotion and fantasy, or tempered by self-interest. A noted nurse and professor of nursing, who spent over four decades caring for sick people and training practitioners, wrote these simple, powerful insights in a book[3] intended for nursing students:

> An individual's religious convictions (that is, his actual beliefs, not those he professes to believe) will strongly influence his ability to cope with suffering when he is undergoing this experience. The individual's actual beliefs are stressed (as opposed to his professed beliefs) *since it is quite one matter to be philosophical about suffering when one is not suffering, and quite another to accept and find meaning in this experience when one is feeling its full impact.*

> In order to [accept suffering and find meaning in it without being crushed by it] an individual must have firmly believed, *as well as followed his religious convictions.* It is improbable (but not impossible) that an individual who has never *practiced* any of his religious beliefs will gain the strength he needs to cope with distress. It is true that some individuals may 'all of a sudden' display an interest in religious matters and seem to derive much strength from these beliefs, but if the individual's 'interest' is not sincere, the force of

these convictions will probably diminish, especially if
. . . he undergoes extreme suffering. The individual who
is able to cope with suffering because of his religious
convictions does not talk as much about his
convictions as he lives them. His [coping] behavior is a
demonstration of beliefs he holds. [Our italics]

In other words, if it is to have meaning, our love of God
and our acceptance of His love must have followed the same
long-term developmental course in life that our steps have
shown to be necessary for the success of human love. We can
dismiss God and His demands, paying lip-service only or
showing more emotionalism, but we shall inevitably reap the
harvest of our misrepresentation of His love: In the moments
when we really need it, our faith in God will not be strong
enough to help us; and His love for us, though always present,
will not be accessible if we are too inexperienced in humility
and too unmindful of our need for God.

To practice the art of loving Our Creator, we must first
understand what love in that context means—what God
gives and what He asks of us. Though eventually we may sense
how God's love animates and sustains us in our life and in our
human loving, we do not start out life with this awareness or
conviction. It may be something we are taught or encounter
early in life—as with the millions of people, the authors
included, who went to Sunday school; or it may be something
we encounter or slowly become aware of much later, at a time
when we are more intellectually, emotionally, and spiritually
conscious. For others, the awareness will happen *very* late in
life, or never become fully conscious at all.

In most cases, however, meaningful encounters with
God's love will take place in the context of a particular

relationship or a group of relationships. God's love for us and the love we show each other in response to it, will occasionally be apparent for many of us in the relationships we have (parent-child, friend-friend, male-female, and so on). We may not recognize this at first, but eventually God's message, and the experience we have directly or through others of God's love, may be perceived.

Sooner or later, in other words, we will become immediately aware of what this love means and what it demands. How we deal with this awareness—whether we confront or avoid it, repress or express it, is another question. It may require months and years to realize what this love offers and what it asks. Both may be rejected, then accepted, then tempered upon, then accepted again. Many of us, indeed most of us, will have to be invited again and again—by the events, thoughts, challenges, crises, demands of our lives—to reconsider the question of God's love and our own loving in the light of that love. But when the moment comes that we are prepared to accept God's love and do our best to respond to it, we shall find that the steps outlined in this book have considerable practical application.

The command of God, whom St. John called "Love," is clear:

> *You shall love the Lord your God with all your heart, and with all your soul, and with all your mind. This is the great and first commandment. And a second is like it, You shall love your neighbor as yourself. On these two commandments depend all the law and the prophets.*
>
> *Matthew 22:37-40*

And the Promise of God to those who would obey is equally direct:

> For I am sure that neither death, nor life, nor angels, nor principalities, nor things present, nor things to come, nor powers, nor height, nor depth, nor anything else in all creation, will be able to separate us from the love of God in Christ Jesus our Lord.
>
> Romans 8:38-39

The words ring out familiarly to everyone in Christendom. They resound magnificently to some, frighteningly to others. But most people are indifferent to them. That these words underpin, infuse, and fulfill the fact and the promise of human love is a possibility that each human being must consider.

For many believers, including the authors, it is impossible to imagine how human love can be ultimately workable and satisfying outside of the meaning of these words—impossible to envision a world where human beings were left entirely alone, dependent upon only their capabilities, where their living and loving ended only in death (figuratively and literally). But it must be conceded that many who do not share this belief make a far better success of their loving than many who do. We have no desire to convert nonbelievers (and we believe that the early chapters of this book have as much to say to them as to the rest). As for those believers who are having troubled love relationships, we would only say that the action of God in your lives is a reminder of the mystery of God's ways, as well as an inspiration and a challenge to bring closer union between our beliefs and our behavior. Finally, we do not believe that the merit, the godliness, if you will, of your loving will be lost

136

through death or through apparent defeat. For those who would now take the rest of the journey with us, we shall attempt to show how the four steps of permanent love apply to our relationship with God and with His community, the Church.

* * *

Step One of loving God focuses on shared activity, which, in this context, means involvement with and commitment to the Body of Christ in the world—the community that is the Church (in the most universal, encompassing sense of the word). From the beginning, Christianity has been a community of faith. This community has been less exclusive than its Judaic ancestor, but the fact that it proclaims its message to the whole world makes it no less intense or close-knit. Faith is not born in a vacuum; nor does it grow and flourish in one. We first encounter the Word of God through the action of the God-centered community. With the collective practice, wisdom, and authority of that community, we develop and hone our faith, preventing its decline into privatism, idolatry, superstition, or illusion. Within that community we learn our first lessons of charity and feed upon the love and support of our fellows for the strength to proclaim the Word outside the community.

The risk here—and you'll recall that each of the steps to permanent love is also a response to society's corruption of love—is that community involvement and commitment will be reduced to empty ritual and routine. No amount of fervor, regularity, or profundity can compensate for an absence or diminution of charity—of *love*—within the community itself. Attending church, receiving the sacraments, and taking in the occasional social function are part, *but only part*, of the shared activity of the Christian community. Precisely because they have become all there is to Step One for many of us, the great emphasis must now be placed on other aspects and possibilities of shared community activity.

And here the best guide, as St. Paul reminds us, is always charity. Where is my active loving most needed? How can it best be expressed within the community of God's people? This may lead to any number of expressions of charity, from showing greater interest in pewmates to participating in more community activity. But the center will reamin your personal, loving involvement with people—service to others in His name, not yours.

I have a close friend who runs a home for "God's poor" and the bedridden. She takes donations as her only means of supporting the eight or so patients she cares for at any one time. I once asked her what her largest donations came to. Rarely more than fifty dollars, she said. Those who give large amounts to charity receive notice in the papers, but not necessarily in God's ledgers.

Are you investing the care and commitment in your loved ones that you invest in other areas of your life? I'm not speaking here of emotional involvement, and this is a crucial point to make. Love, as we saw, is primarily an *act* of will. Emotions often accompany it, as do appetites; but they do not control it. What the Christian community needs and requires from you is not, therefore, an increase of effulgent feelings, but your calm, considered *willingness* to give your love-commitment high priority.

Step Two—what you can do on your own—is as crucial

in loving God as it is in building enduring relationships with your fellow human beings. For although the Christian faith is structured fundamentally on the community, its message and concern concentrates on the individual. There can be no lasting, authentic religious faith that is not intensely personal, carved sometimes out of doubt, confusion, fear, apathy, and insecurity by the person himself. The *responsibility* of maintaining and deepening faith, of acting it out in love, is the individual's. If the person looks to the community to carry him along, that is, to do his affirming and loving for him, then he weakens the community and himself.

Thus, one of the most important things a Christian can do for his relationship with God and with the Church is to strengthen himself by working alone at affirming his faith and (inevitably) perfecting his charity. In the context of faith and charity, Step Two translates into aligning your own actions closer to the example of Christ, *regardless of the response of other people or even (as you perceive it) of God himself.* Step Two is *learning to do*, regardless of how you feel, how you fear, or how others react. It means having and developing the willingness to act for love when love does not seem to be acting for you. The analogy between your human lover and God may seem to break down at this point, since you know beforehand that God loves you eternally, whereas your lover, being human, may well walk away. But the whole point about the love of God is that while His love is indeed eternal, *your awareness of it and your acceptance of it are, to you in the here-and-now, very often absent.* When you do not see or feel His love, your intellectual knowledge that it is there nonetheless, offers slight consolation.

Step Two is the vital component that we too often forget in our pursuit of a relationship with God. Too often,

139

we, like Betty, abdicate our responsibility to work at loving Him, and therefore our loving and our faith are weakened. Just as there are many, many counter-loving forces in us and in society that pull us apart from our human loved ones, so there are many more that separate us from our love of God and our acceptance of His love for us. Only we can work at overcoming these obstacles (since we created them). Often that will mean working alone and in near despair, for we feel unloved. All we seem to have to go on, then, is our own capacity to love, which we must cling to and improve despite our failure and fear. It is then that you still must act on your own, as indeed Our Lord Himself did on the cross. Step Two may well lead you to your soul's dark night, but only in persevering *on your own* will you find the dawn; only then will you discover that you never were, never are, never will be "on your own."

Step Three—conversation—is very simple in the context of loving God: it means prayer. Prayer is absolutely, uniquely vital to the relationship one has with God. There are several varieties of prayer such as thanksgiving, confession, petition, and praise. And there are nearly as many ways of praying as there are occasions to pray. But this is not the place to describe them all. Prayer, like conversation, does not need to be sophisticated or advanced to be meaningful. On the contrary, like conversation, it must flow naturally out of the unfolding process of one's life. Prayer does not serve to keep God informed about our lives. (Can Tom Sawyer tell Mark Twain anything he doesn't already know?) Prayer should instead keep *us* mindful of His presence and hence open to the possibility of His participation in our lives. Prayer makes our involvement with God meaningful in a direct way that nothing else can do—not interaction with people, not taking the sacraments, not thought and reflection, not reading scripture (as *important* as all these activities are).[4]

The corruption of Step Three in loving God corresponds to what we earlier called communication—an overemphasis on transmitting and receiving feelings at the expense of content and shared activity. In the religious realm, one could speak of the emotionalization or even eroticization of faith and point to some of the popular cults and movements of our day as examples of this corruption. The significant service these groups have rendered the institutional churches by way of loosening the stifling grip of ritual and tradition has been seriously offset by the baneful reduction of faith to emotional ecstasy and of charity to obtuse proselytizing.

Emotions should not be excluded from the worship of God, from faith and religion, any more than feelings can or should be excluded from human relationships. In neither realm, however, should we permit feelings to become the central experience, goal, and standard of reference. Emotion is a spurious shortcut to the Almighty. As C. S. Lewis expresses in the following excerpt from his book about the death of his wife (*A Grief Observed*), in the final analysis, emotion and love part ways. The author is speaking of a presentiment he has just experienced of his dead wife, Helen:

> [Generally] the absence of emotion [from love] repelled me. But in this contact (whether real or apparent) it didn't do anything of the sort. One didn't need emotion. The intimacy was complete—sharply bracing and restorative too—without it. Can that intimacy be love itself—always in this life attended with emotion, not because it is itself an emotion, or needs an

attendant emotion, but because our animal souls, our nervous systems, our imaginations, have to respond to it in that way? If so, how many preconceptions I must scrap![5]

Step Four—working out difficulties—leads us to the consideration of pain. "Evil and unhappiness are the rocks upon which all arguments for the existence of God must finally come to wreck," writes one clear-seeing theologian[6] summarizing the traditional attack on Christianity by those (like the philosopher David Hume) who argue that if God is good, and if He is omnipotent, there should be no evil in the world. God and religion play a major role in the lives of many clients, lay and clergy, with whom I've worked during my years of counseling. These people (and the rest of us who struggle consciously to be Christian) have to withstand any number of internal and external attacks on faith—from science, psychology, sociology, abusive authority, doubt, failure. Some believers succumb to these sieges; most do not. The greatest attack on traditional religious faith, however— the one that time and again I have seen temporarily undermine even the strongest faith (my own included)—is the occurrence in a person's life of some grave misfortune or series of misfortunes. "Why me, Lord?" rises the plaint to heaven. "Why, if I have kept the faith, am I taking this pasting? How can You do this to Your loyal servant, me?"

Unforeseen and undesired events and situations occur regularly in the course of our lives. We are individually or collectively responsible for creating some of them—such as pollution, bad government, the breakup of love relationships, or the turning to drugs. In other cases, such as the aging process, illness, death, natural catastrophes, we have no control whatever. As in Step Four, where we discussed problem solving in the context of human love, here, too, the process of working out difficulties must hinge upon the crucial question of *responsibility*. Where the difficulty in question is one that we caused or helped to cause, we must take our share of the responsibility for it and begin immediately the process of rectifying what is wrong (which may entail either individual or group effort). If this seems simplistic, I would invite you to step into my office (or the office of any other counselor, teacher, or minister) and listen to the blame-ducking that issues, obviously or subtly, from the mouths of just about everyone. The secular-minded or the agnostic scatter responsibility for their self-inflicted woes onto other people; the more religious types often arraign the Almighty. The result is the same: personal responsibility is evaded; the job of working the problem out (that is, changing) is shifted to someone else.

But what about misfortunes over which we have no control? Many of them (disease, death, drought, flood, senility, and so forth) are part of the course of human life, and we should expect and be prepared for them. The point is—and it's fundamental—God does not promise us immunity from pain and suffering in this life. Much as we might desire continual happiness, He does not indicate that unalloyed happiness is a realistic or even desirable goal for us. What He does promise is "to be with you always, even unto the end of the earth." That Presence, while not guaranteeing lasting pleasure or gratification, does offer inner joy, strength, and peace if we will but accept these gifts.

Learning to accept them entails (among other things) our accepting the responsibility for what we can control and tolerating philosophically the bad and the good for which we

143

are not responsible. Philosophical acceptance, by the way, implies a measure of personal responsibility in managing one's own reaction to events. In one sense, this is the place where Step Four in practicing the love of God does not seem to correspond directly with Step Four in human love. At a certain point it would appear that it is not possible for us to understand every difficulty and play a role in working it out. Furthermore, submission to the will of God has no direct counterpart in our human relationships.

On the other hand, as you may have discovered in working out difficulties within the context of human love relationships, there arrives periodically a point at which difficulties cannot finally be understood and totally resolved by both parties. In every human being there is an element of absolute mystery and "otherness"—as unknowable to the person himself as to his lover. "Sometimes I just can't understand my wife/husband," we so often hear. In the course of human loving, although much more can be done than we usually do to eradicate upset, pain, and suffering and to advance our mutual understanding, responsibility, confidence, and control, there are ultimately limits. These limits appear most overtly, of course, in our dealings with friends and lovers. Thus, as important and helpful as Step Four is, there will nonetheless be occasions when it must blend back into Step Two—that is, when we have done all we can do in tandem to work out difficulties, when the limits have been reached; then the remaining work must be our own inner work of acceptance and submission.

Our friend Betty was obviously beginning to encounter difficulties in distinguishing between what she was and was not responsible for. In certain areas, such as reducing her unrealistic expectations of her children and her husband, she should have accepted her responsibility, but she chose not to. Instead, she lived partially with fantasy and illusion and shifted part of the blame to other shoulders when her unrealistic hopes were not met. In other areas, such as growing older or having her friends become ill and die, Betty struggled unconsciously to control events, to have responsibility for them. And when she could not, she was again frustrated and embittered.

I don't wish to belabor Betty's example. She wasn't doing anything that all of us periodically don't do, or aren't strongly tempted to do. At such times our love of God comes into play, along with the effort that we put into developing it. Betty had reached her human limits. After several decades of giving the best human loving she could, she was just tired out. If she had put the same vigilance and vitality into practicing her love of God that she had put into her love of people (instead of letting her faith become routinized and empty), she would then have had the peace and strength she needed to fall back upon. She would have experienced God's love, and this would have enabled her to show increased, instead of decreased, charity at a time in her life when she felt she could give no more.

This, in effect, is what the steps do in the context of loving God: They permit us to accept the awesome, unbelievable fact that God loves us and that His love, in the words of the old Anglican Book of Common Prayer, is "full, perfect, and sufficient" in a way that no human love can ever be. This realization both expands and deepens our human love relationships by enabling us to show greater charity; and yet it detaches us from overdependence on, or false expectations for, the objects of our human love. Not needing human love *quite* so desperately, we are paradoxically far better able to love and to serve in our human relationships. And, basking in the joy and peace of God's love, we are far better placed to tolerate the inevitable suffering and limits of human life.

* * *

Finally, there is no avoiding the fact that human love, as it moves toward permanence, tends inexorably in the direction of charity, charity, and more charity. In the context of ongoing life as we human beings have created it—the *only* context where real love can exist—the ground is not fundamentally congenial to self-interested, emotional, appetite-dominated loving. This kind of loving will only be frustrated and turned back on itself. The relationships it gives birth to will die again and again; they will not endure because the ground of life will not feed them. Only as we feed our relationships with increasing amounts of charity will they endure in the long run. But there are limits to our capacity for self-giving if we do not finally raise our eyes to the direction in which love points and whence it comes.

NOTES:

[1]There is one major exception to what I've said regarding loving and being loved. As infants and young children, we are in great need of the abundant, unquestioning, forgiving love of our parents (or whoever cares for us). Childhood is the one time of life when it is more important for us to be loved than to love, for the simple reason that we do not yet know how to love. Parental love is the supreme example of love given unconditionally, pointing the way to our own loving as we mature. See *For the Love of Children*, chap. 9.

[2]See C. S. Lewis, *The Four Loves*, p. 156.

[3]Joyce Travelbee, *Interpersonal Aspects of Nursing* (Philadelphia: F. A. Davis Co., 1966), pp. 65, 70-72.

[4]The exception to this statement might be the mystical union with God that extraordinary men and women like Meister Eckhart, John of the Cross, or Theresa of Avila speak of in their writings. Like most people, I was strongly tempted to write off mysticism as a viable and accessible means of loving God. Then I read a simple, digestible book by Evelyn Underhill aptly titled *Practical Mysticism*. I urge you to read it.

[5]C. S. Lewis, *A Grief Observed* (New York: Bantam Books, 1976), p. 58.

[6]M. Holmes Hartshorne, *The Faith To Doubt* (Englewood Cliffs, N.J.: Prentice Hall, Inc., 1963), p. 62.

ABOUT THE AUTHORS:

Ed Ford is an associate and resident faculty member of the Institute for Reality Therapy of Los Angeles. He consults, lectures, and teaches counseling techniques in Reality Therapy in schools, universities, mental health and correctional facilities, hospitals, businesses, alcohol, drug, and rehabilitation centers, youth homes, and U.S. military bases. He gives courses and workshops throughout the Southwest on marriage, raising children, and handling stress. In one recent application, he developed a program of marriage preparation for the Catholic Diocese of Youngstown, Ohio. He is the author of three other books based on Reality Therapy: *Why Marriage?*, *Why Be Lonely?*, and *For the Love of Children*. He and his wife, Hester, are the parents of eight children and live in Scottsdale, Arizona.

Steven Englund is a former correspondent for the "Behavior" section of *Time*. His work has also appeared in the London *Times* literary supplement, the *New York Times*, the *New York Review of Books*, and other publications. Co-author with Ed Ford of *For the Love of Children*, he has taught at UCLA and published on diverse topics such as French government and history, the American film industry, and the nature of violence in American family life. When not on assignment, he makes his home in Waupaca, Wisconsin.

148